I dedicate this book to my wonderful wife, Ginny. Thank you for your support and for your help in writing this book, but more than that, thank you for living communication with me, every day. Not only do you understand the skills and teach the skills yourself, but you personify the skills every day, as a living example.

— Jacob Weisberg

DOES ANYBODY LISTEN?
DOES ANYBODY CARE?

By Jacob Weisberg

DOES ANYBODY LISTEN?
DOES ANYBODY CARE?

Author:
Jacob Weisberg
President
Creative Communications
P.O. Box 776
Trabuco Canyon, CA 92679
(714) 589-1723

Published by:
Medical Group Management Association
104 Inverness Terrace East
Englewood, CO 80112
(303) 799-1111

Table of Contents

Chapter ten — Asking Questions............................ 101

Chapter eleven — Responding to Questions 117

Chapter twelve — Silence 129

Epilogue 135

Acknowledgments

Nothing happens in a vacuum.

The material contained in this book never could have been written were it not for the experiences I had, the schooling I took and the mentoring, advice and influences on me by so many people.

In essence, if you ever were employed in the same organization as I was, thank you — you influenced this book.

If you were ever on the same committee with me, thank you — you influenced this book.

If you ever were any of my instructors at school — thank you. Sorry I gave you grief then, but you certainly influenced this book.

If you ever were in any of the classes or seminars I offered, thank you — you influenced this book.

But in addition to the virtual world at large that played a role in this book, there are certain people who got inside my life, inside my head and inside my activities — and these people really gave me the impetus to write the book. I must recognize them now.

To **Mike** and **Peter Gotfredson** and **Drew Kaplan**, for allowing me the opportunity to extend the application of communication skills to the world of commerce.

To **Stacy Weichhart** and **Amy Reece** for allowing me the opportunity to extend the application of communication skills to the world of public utilities.

To **Mark Howard, Suresh, Joe Hegenbart, Ken Kasner, Cynthia Carter, Vivian Minot** and **Paul Shockley** for allowing me the opportunity to extend the application of communication skills to the world of a governmental department.

To **Hal Prink** for allowing me the opportunity to extend the application of the skills to the world of medical management.

To **John Harbourne, Bill Rush** and **Bruce Brenholdt** for allowing me the opportunity to extend the application of communication skills to their medical groups.

To **Doris Kasold** for allowing me the opportunity to extend the application of communication to the world of mass media.

To **Bill Richardson, Paul Brooks** and **Dan Gryder** for allowing me the opportunity to extend the application of communication to the world of the pharmaceutical industry.

To **Neil, Judy, Claire, Carol, Lee, Connie, Anita, Ruth, Bayla** and **Marcia**, my co-leaders at the Institute, who taught me how to understand communication skills better, and gave me the opportunity to extend the application of communication skills into the community at large.

To my wonderful children who often prove that no amount of communication training is enough and to my 14 grandchildren who have a way of bringing me back to earth and helping me realize that just when I think I've learned how to communicate, there's a new language springing up, a new style of communicating and that I'd better get started learning all over again.

I also appreciate the help of the Medical Group Management staff members: **Fred E. Graham, II, Ph.D.**, senior associate executive director; **Dennis L. Barnhardt, APR**, director of communications; **Barbara U. Hamilton**, library resource center director; **Brenda E. Hull**, communications project manager; **Stephanie S. Wyllyamz**, communications specialist; **Sheila A. Tuitele**, communications advertising specialist; **Ellie J. Cox**, communications administrative secretary; and **Cynthia M. Kiyotake**, librarian.

About the Author

Jacob Weisberg is president of Creative Communications. He frequently consults and speaks on listening and communications bottlenecks in organizations. He teaches skills that help people work more efficiently and more cooperatively with both internal and external colleagues, staff, patients, clients or customers.

Prior to founding his own company he enjoyed a career in the health care industry, first with Ayerst Laboratories, Division of American Home Products, as division manager. At West Chemical Products he was the director of the Germicide Division and then became vice president.

Weisberg has a master's of business administration from Pepperdine University, Malibu, Calif., which followed undergraduate work in chemistry and education at Fordham University, New York, N.Y.

He is involved with the American Society for Training and Development, and has held office in the American Medical Writers Association and the National Speakers Association. He is listed as an authority on listening and communication skills in the *Yearbook of Experts, Authorities and Spokespersons*. He has written numerous articles on medical and general management.

Prologue

"Sit down and don't say a word.
We're going to COMMUNICATE!"

"Communication is the most
important skill in life."

Stephen R. Covey,
The 7 Habits of Highly Effective People

"I love my doctor." That's what many patients say and they prove it by their willingness to go anywhere to follow their doctor. On the other hand, other patients leave a practice just because they don't like their doctor.

"I think I get treated just fine," is what some patients say about the medical group practices where they seek care. "I shudder every time I think I have to go there," is what other patients say about the way they're treated at their facility.

Complaining patients ...
Disgruntled patient ...
Frustrated employees ...

"I enjoy the work atmosphere, my relationships with my colleagues and supervisors," say some employees and they reflect that to the patients. "I hate coming to work, can't stand my boss or the work environment," is what other employees say.

Three different scenarios, yet all affect the success of any medical group — your medical group. Is there one single secret that can convert these unhappy and frustrated expressions to ones of pleasure? Probably not, but there probably is a common thread connecting them. That thread is one of communications.

Complaining patients did not know how to complain or to whom to complain. Maybe they did complain and did not feel listened to. There was a lack of communication, or the communication channel was not open.

Disgruntled patients did not like the way they were treated and didn't know how to get that changed. Communication again.

Frustrated employees did not know their options, knew them but didn't know how to use them or did not feel comfortable using them. They couldn't communicate and hadn't been communicated with.

If communication lies at the core of these scenarios, and hundreds of other scenarios played out daily at group practices across the country, then it becomes obvious that attention must be paid to the *skills* of communication.

"Skills? What skills? Communication isn't a skill, it's natural." That's what so many people believe. We're born with it. After all, babies don't study communication skills and they communicate.

This is true. In fact, it has sometimes been said that communication is perfectly natural and in infancy is even naturally perfect. But, as we mature, instead of building on this heritage, we corrupt it, so that the clear messages an infant sent are no longer as clear, direct and innocent when that infant enters adulthood.

What, then, are the skills that can help us communicate more clearly, more directly and more acceptably?

First, let us define communication. We define it as a two-way exchange of facts, thoughts or ideas and feelings or emotions by the written word, spoken word or body language.

Please note that communication is two way. If one person is doing all the talking and the other all the listening, it's not communication, it's a monologue.

Employees don't consider it communication when their boss says to them, "Sit down. Don't say anything. I don't want to hear a word from you. We're going to communicate." That's positional power, not communication.

Patients don't consider it communication when their doctor says to them, "Let's talk about it," and then the doctor does all the talking, leaves no room for questions or comments and leaves. Patients don't consider it communication when an employee issues instructions for a procedure without checking to see if there's been understanding.

Communication takes place in many ways — the written word and the kind of paper it's written on, the spoken word and the tone of voice that sends the message, the facial expression that signals doubt or the smile that signals pride — they are all part of communication.

When we communicate we have four needs which we desperately want fulfilled. In marketing it has been said, "Find a need and fill it." Medical groups search for niches and departments search for ways to serve the patient's needs. Yet, they sometimes lose sight that when they're with the patient, the patient has the following four needs, above and beyond their clinical needs. If these four communication needs are filled, the patient will be happy, and they'll even be more tolerant of failures to meet their clinical needs.

What are these four communication needs?

- The need to feel listened to;
- The need to feel understood;
- The need to know the other person's opinion; and
- The need for closure.

The need to feel listened to

That's an emotional need, one that gets satisfied or is left hungering based on what we say, what we do and how we behave. The skill of active listening caters to that need.

The need to feel understood

After a person feels listened to (and only after they feel listened to) do they feel the need to be understood. The skill of paraphrasing caters to that need.

The need to know the other person's point of view

How we enter the conversation, what we say and how we say it, will affect the success of the communication. Many communication skills are brought into play now.

The need for closure

People don't like things to be left hanging. Even bad news is better than the "unknown." So how do we break the bad news? How do we tell them the good news? How do we tell them the results are not in yet, and that they have to wait? More communications skills are:

- active listening;
- buying time;
- paraphrasing;
- reverse paraphrasing;
- asking questions;
- answering questions;
- use of "I";
- use of "you";
- fact description;
- expression of feelings;
- reflection of feelings;
- words and music; and
- silence.

"People don't like things to be left hanging."

And the corollaries are:

- How to enter a conversation;
- How to disagree without fighting;
- How to give instructions and be sure they're understood;
- How to give bad news;
- How to give good news; and
- The secret of "I" and "you" in marketing.

Communication needs

Feel _____

Feel _____

Know _____

And finally _____

CHAPTER ONE

Active Listening

"But doctor, you don't LOOK
like you're listening."

"Most people do not listen with the intent to understand, they listen with the intent to reply. They're either speaking or preparing to speak. They're filtering everything through their own paradigms, reading their autobiography into other people's lives."

Stephen R. Covey, The 7 Habits of Highly Effective People

This skill caters to the other person's number one need — the need to feel listened to. When they feel listened to, they feel good. They are more willing to cooperate.

If they're a patient, they go home saying, "My doctor listens to me," "My nurse listens to me" or "Those wonderful people at the front desk, they're so nice."

If they're employees, they tell their friends, "I like working at my group, my boss is such a nice person." Not only that, these employees reflect their own satisfaction in their exchanges with the patients.

"Hold on there, Jacob," said one person at a workshop I led recently, "What's this reference to active listening. Why don't you just call it listening? After all," he continued, "I don't have to really do anything to listen, except to keep my ears open. It's your job as the speaker to speak loud enough so that my hearing system hears it."

That's the point. The hearing system is one thing — listening is another. If you do nothing but keep your ears open, that's hearing. But, the speaker still may not feel listened to. There's more to active listening than keeping your ears open. It is an activity. You do have to work at it.

"There's more to active listening than keeping your ears open."

But, is it worth it? Is it worth keeping employees happy? Is it worth building outstanding working relationships with your colleagues? Is it worth having patients recommend your group to others?

Okay, okay. But those are just empty claims — prove it!

Let me start by painting a picture and sharing a part of my life with you. It's not important where this event took place, nor when, but take my word for it — this is real, it happened to me, it changed my life, it has changed the lives of hundreds, no, thousands of others and may very well change your life too.

I was working with a family, a husband, wife and two teenage children, one boy and one girl, that was having trouble "communicating." They said they loved each other and that as long as conversations were focused on telling each other how much they loved and cared about each other, there was no communication problem.

If they discussed superficial matters there were still no problems, but when they got to matters of significance or disagreement, that's when love flew out the window. Anger and frustration crept in and destroyed their entire communication process. My job was to help them by teaching them communication skills and how to use them.

To better understand their situation and help me make my instruction specific to their everyday lives, we arranged for me to come to their home and spend a weekend (Friday evening until Sunday night) with them — to see what happened 24 hours a day.

This was a new experience for me. Though I recognized the importance of this activity, I was nervous. It's one thing to teach in a classroom or even in a living room environment. It's quite another thing to move in and live with the family and become part of that environment.

This was also somewhat uncomfortable for the family. After all, it's one thing to go a class — it's another thing to bring the teacher into the house and live with him, exposing all the inner workings of family life. But, we were all committed. I cleared my calendar, they cleared theirs. We were committed to 48 hours together.

Friday evening came. They welcomed me to their home and showed me to a wonderful guest room. When I came downstairs, we talked. There was good communication — what a relief. They were nervous, so was I. Everyone was on their best behavior. I thought to myself, "This is going to work out just fine."

As the weekend wore on I noticed some cracks in the communication process. I made some notes so that I would really be able to hone in on the specifics when we got back to

"'Normal' reared its ugly head Sunday morning."

class. The nervousness was beginning to wear away — they got used to me and I got used to them. I almost became a part of the woodwork, and it was then that their communication and behavior patterns returned to normal.

"Normal" reared its ugly head Sunday morning. We had just finished breakfast when the man of the house went into the family room to read the Sunday paper. I had nothing to see or do at that moment so I followed him into the family room and sat off in a corner to relax.

Then his wife came into the room. She was in a good mood. They were going on an overseas vacation soon, and she was anxious to tell him about her ideas of what to do while they were there and what still had to be done before they left. Her voice and smile showed her excitement and enthusiasm about the upcoming trip.

"You know, honey, it's getting closer to our vacation, and the kids and I are so excited. I hope you're excited too. I've already started making plans and have taken care of lots of things, but there are still some things that are pending. I sure would like your help with them.

"For example, you know that my car isn't working too well. I sure would like to get it fixed. And Billie needs his braces tightened before we go. Can you make the appointment with the orthodontist, he's your friend. Jane needs her allergy shots. Should we go back to the last allergist we used, or should we find a new one who is closer?

"Talking about shots, we don't have all of our shots yet. When will get them? Where will we get them?

"We've all got our passports, but we don't yet have all the visas we need. Weren't you handling that?

"Let's tell the neighbors the exact dates we'll be away so they can look after the house.

"We need to tell the newspaper boy to stop delivering until we get back, and we must tell the gardeners everything they need to do while we are gone.

"And Aunt May. You know, years ago she lived in Europe. Let's go visit her at the nursing home and tell her about our trip. She'll be so excited. It will bring her such pleasure. And she may even have friends there she wants us to look up or call."

She was so happy to be sharing all this excitement with him, but he kept reading his paper, never looked up, never said anything — he just kept reading.

> "She was going to make sure he heard, so she repeated."

She was going to make sure he heard, so repeated:

"You know, honey, it's getting closer to our trip, and the kids and I are so excited. I hope you're excited too. I've already started making plans and have taken care of lots of things, but there are still some things that are pending. I sure would like your help with them.

"For example, you know that my car isn't working too well. I sure would like to get it fixed. And Billie needs his braces tightened before we go. Can you make the appointment with the orthodontist? He's your friend. Jane needs her allergy shots. Should we go back to the last allergist we used or should we find a new one who is closer?

"Talking about shots, we don't have all of our shots yet. When will get them? Where will we get them?

"We've all got our passports, but we don't yet have all the visas we need. Weren't you handling that?

"Let's tell the neighbors the exact dates we'll be away so they can look after the house.

"We need to tell the newspaper boy to stop delivering until we get back. And we must tell the gardeners everything they need to do while we are gone.

"And Aunt May. You know, years ago she lived in Europe. Let's go visit her at the nursing home and tell her about our trip. She'll be so excited. It will bring her such pleasure. And she may even have friends there she wants us to look up or call."

He continued reading, and she continued talking. But, now her disposition had begun to change.

Before, she was standing at the doorway, smiling and happy. Now, her voice was raised and she was moving closer to him as she repeated the same message over and over.

And he kept reading the newspaper.

She kept repeating, her voice growing more shrill, her face contorting in anger. She looked at him, then at me, then back at him. She kept getting closer and closer to him, now virtually screaming the message at the top of her lungs. Finally, in total frustration, she slammed her fist into the newspaper, knocking it from his hands sending it flying in all directions. She looked at him and in total frustration, annoyance and exhaustion said, "You didn't hear one word I said, not one word!"

She turned to me and said, "You see, that's the problem in our relationship. He doesn't listen." Then she added, "Fix him and we'll be okay."

I was stunned. I was not prepared for the scene I had just witnessed, nor was I prepared for her comment directed toward me. I didn't know what to say, but I did know the skill of silence, so I said nothing. And he came to my rescue.

> "You didn't hear one word I said, not one word."

His paper had just been knocked from his hands all over the floor. He looked up at his wife in disbelief, and then looked around at the newspaper — his wife — at the paper, finally directing his attention to the newspaper.

He got on his hands and knees and began gathering the pages together. All the while his wife stood over him, panting, almost frothing, waiting for him to say something.

He said nothing, just kept putting the paper together.

She was in turmoil. She knew it wouldn't end with him just putting the paper together. Sooner or later he would say something and she was waiting — waiting for him to speak.

Finally, he looked up at her and said, "Oh yeah? You told me you were excited about the trip. Well, I'm excited too. You also said you were concerned about several aspects of it."

He continued, very derisively, "First, you were concerned about the visas. Yes, we do need visas and you're right, I am handling it. So what are you so uptight about? The applications have already been sent in. If I don't hear from them within a week, I'll be back in touch with them.

"Second, you were concerned about the shots we need. Why are you asking me? You usually make the medical appointments. Find out from our travel agent what shots we need, call our doctor, tell him what shots we need and make an appointment. You know my schedule. What's the fuss all about?"

He became more sarcastic as he continued, "Third, Billie and his orthodontia. There is no need for me to handle that, that's Billie's concern. He knows his braces are loose. He knows his dentist's phone number. He's always handled those things himself, what's the fuss now?

"Fourth, Jane. She drives her own car, manages to get all over town to do what she wants to do, so she could easily get to her allergist on her own. If she doesn't want to go to that allergist, she could check with her friends to find out who they would recommend. Why should we even get involved? She's a young lady now, let her handle it herself. If that's not okay with you, then you make all the decisions for her, you drive her around, but you leave me out of it."

He beamed with pleasure, "Fifth, your car. What do you want from me? Call the dealership and tell them the problem. Tell them that they told you last time they would need the car for several days and now they can have it for two weeks. I don't see what you're so upset about, or why you're even telling me.

"What's next? Oh yeah, Aunt May. Great idea. Let's go see her. You're right, she probably will get a lot of pleasure from hearing about our trip. But don't just talk about it, let's do it. I can't do it today but how about next Sunday?

"And then the neighbors — tell them! What do you want from me? The gardener — you're always dealing with him anyhow, tell him whatever you want to. The newspaper, sure. Just call the newspaper circulation office — there's an 800 number in every issue — and tell them what day to discontinue and when to start again. And by the way," he chortled, "You forgot to mention the mail. I'll drop by the post office and fill out a form to have them suspend delivery while we're away and hold our mail."

"I heard every word she said."

Finally, in total triumph he yelled, "Now tell me I didn't hear one word you said."

Then he looked at me and added, "I heard every word she said. What does she want from me? Fix her, we'll be okay!"

Again, I was dumbfounded and caught by surprise. What could I say?

I didn't have to say anything, so silence worked again. This time, she came to my rescue.

There she was, excited, hyperventilating, annoyed, angry and shaking, for it was obvious to her that he had heard every word she said. As she later told me, not only had he heard every word she said, he had heard it, understood it, integrated it and repeated it back to her in a more logical order than she had given it to him, adding his own views as well. "What was still worse," she said to me, "is that there had been a witness present — you." Then she gathered her thoughts, her feelings and her energy as she said to him the words that

"Well, you didn't look like you were listening."

literally changed my life, changed the lives of thousands of people who have participated in our seminars and workshops, and will undoubtedly change the lives of many who read this book. She said, "Oh yeah? Well you didn't look like you were listening." You didn't look like you were listening.

You see, to her it was more important to feel listened to than it was to be understood.

Her emotional need was to be validated as a person, to have that inner part of her know that she was important, and she didn't get that from the exchange with her husband.

It didn't matter that he had heard every word she said. It didn't matter that he could integrate everything she said. It didn't matter that he could remember and repeat it all back to her. Her primary communication need had not been met. She did not feel listened to and the communication could not take place without it.

So the question now becomes, what could he have done, what should he have done to give his wife that feeling of being listened to?

That is the skill of active listening.

And now you see — it is active. He must do something. He can't just sit there and hear.

There are four components to the skill of active listening:

- eye contact;
- body posture;
- verbal acknowledgment; and
- appropriate facial expression.

Eye contact

Look at her. Put down the newspaper and look at her. That validates her, gives her a feeling of importance.

"But what if the speaker doesn't look at me?" ask seminar participants. No matter, keep looking at them. If they gaze out the window, keep looking at them. If they stare at the ceiling, keep looking at them. Even if they walk and talk, sometimes turning their back to you, keep looking at them. They'll turn, just you wait, and when they do, you'll be there, eyes on them, to greet them. They'll feel listened to.

And when they feel listened to they feel good, and they feel good about you. They'll be more apt to return and meet their next appointment. They'll be more apt to be compliant with their routine for medication. They'll be more apt to recommend your facility to others. In fact, don't be surprised if they rave with praise about it.

Body posture

Lean forward. When you lean forward you convey a message to them of "connection." It says to them, "I'm with you." Notice, it doesn't say I agree, or disagree, it just says, "You're important enough for me to devote myself to you. I'm here. I'm with you. I'm connected to you."

So, if you're sitting, sit at the front edge of the seat, leaning forward, toward the speaker. If you're standing, regardless of the amount of space between you, lean forward slightly.

What about on the telephone?

Wonderful observation. Neither of the preceding components can be utilized on the phone. The speaker can't see what we're looking at, nor can he or she see how we're leaning. (This will change as the technology for video phones overtakes us. In the future patients will be able to see us, and we'll be able to see them. Even when talking to our colleague down the hall, we'll have a visual connection. Then both of the above components will be universal.)

But for now, since the first two components are not applicable, the two that follow become even more important.

Verbal acknowledgment

Whether you're face to face or on the phone, the speaker needs to hear you to feel listened to. The speaker doesn't necessarily want agreement or disagreement, the speaker just wants to see that you're listening, hear that you're listening. We offer that with sounds of verbal acknowledgment.

Sounds? What kinds of sounds?

We say things like:

- "uh huh";
- "oh";
- "I see";
- "I understand";
- "wow";
- "interesting"; and
- "oh my."

The list is almost endless. Notice, we don't say "yes," and we don't say "no." Some people take these as signs of agreement or disagreement, and they're not asking for our opinion yet.

They just want to feel listened to. Of course the ultimate of verbal acknowledgment is, "Tell me more" or "Keep talking" or "And then what happened?" Notice, in all cases, the listener connects and asks the speaker to keep going.

How different this is from normal "communication" where each person is just waiting for the other person to take a breath so that the listener can now become the speaker. Many people only tolerate the speaking of the other person because they are polite and they're waiting for their turn to speak. It's sometimes called "communication ping pong." You speak, I don't listen, but I'm polite and don't interrupt. But, first chance I get, it's my turn. Then I speak but you don't listen. It's very polite, but not very satisfying.

How different you will be when you're an active listener. Instead of trying to take the ball away from the other person, instead of patiently or impatiently waiting for them to finish, you'll be devoted to them, helping them feel listened to.

They don't get that feeling very often from too many other people, sadly — maybe from nobody else. When they get it from you they'll sing your praises and the praises of your facility.

As important as 'verbal acknowledgment' is in face-to-face conversation, it is most important where eye contact and body posture are not available. On the phone, verbal acknowledgment becomes the most important.

Have you ever been on the phone talking with someone but not hearing anything from them, and wondering if they were still there?

Maybe you did what so many people have told me they do. Some people actually ask, "Hello, are you there? Anybody home?" Of course this happens. The speaker's primary need is to feel listened to, and if they don't get it, they'll turn heaven and earth to get it.

So when you're the listener, give it to them — that feeling of being listened to.

Appropriate facial expression. < Smile, frown or neutral, depending on what's being said. >

When the speaker says something funny, it's okay — smile, laugh. They love it. They see it as a connection and they feel listened to. When the speaker says something sad, it's okay to frown. Once again they love it. They see it as a connection, and they feel listened to. Keep a neutral face, of course, if neither happy nor sad is being said.

And yes, these facial expressions can be heard on the phone. The other person can literally see/hear your smile and see/hear your frown, so let them have what they so desperately need — to feel listened to.

If the husband in our example had put down his paper, looked at his wife, leaned towards her, uttered verbal acknowledgments and smiled or frowned as appropriate, there would have been a totally different outcome. She would have felt listened to.

I am often asked, "But what about him and his rights? Just because she wants to talk, does he have to listen? Isn't he entitled to read his paper?"

Yes, he is entitled, and just because she wants to talk doesn't mean he has to listen, but in that case, there's another skill which needs to be employed (we'll learn that later). He can't just keep reading and "ignore" her.

For now, let's agree that when another person talks to us we'll devote ourselves to listening. In my view there is no such thing as a part-time listener. When you talk to me, you own me 100 percent. Please repeat that and make it your motto! When you talk to me, you own me 100 percent!

Sadly, most people do not feel listened to when they communicate with others. That's why it's such a common complaint of:

- wives about their husbands;
- husbands about their wives;
- children about their parents;
- parents about their children;
- employers about their employees; and
- employees about their supervisors.

And in our domain:

- patients about their physicians;
- patients about medical and hospital employees; and
- staff about colleagues.

If it's such a common complaint (and it is) and the skill to combat it is so simple to implement, then why isn't it being used more often?

Because we've never been taught!

Consider your own academic training — reading, writing and 'rithmatic — with nothing in regards to communication.

No, I'm not against those skills. I'm a writer myself. I do a tremendous amount of reading and I can add a column of figures, but I am amazed that with all of my academic training and with all of the academic training of so many people in the health care profession that so much time was spent on these skills and so little time on learning how to speak and even less time on learning how to listen. Oh sure, we've been told, "You've got to listen," but nobody ever taught us *how*. We've been told, "Speak nicely," but nobody ever taught us what specific words have what specific affect on others. So let's stop wondering about why we might not have utilized these components of active listening until now, and vow that we will from now on.

At this point in a seminar someone usually asks, "But what if I don't have time to listen now? What if I'm charting? What if I'm on my way to a meeting? What if I just don't want to listen?"

Yes, there will be many times when a patient will be telling you things and you need to record it, be it clinical data, financial data or family data. Ideally, you listen and write later. However, I recognize this is not always possible or practical. That's when we "buy time," (a skill we'll learn later) but for now, let's agree, that under most circumstances, when they talk to you, they own you 100 percent.

Others ask, "What if the circumstances prevent active listening?" If I'm operating in the operating room, no matter what's being said to me, I can't give them eye contact. If I'm driving the car, I can't be giving eye contact to the speaker. If I'm eating I better make sure I watch my fork rather than the speaker. What now?"

Separate sets of circumstances require separate responses.

When the situation prevents active listening (in the operating room, in the car) the speaker knows this, and there is a virtual unwritten agreement that active listening is suspended.

Some former students have told me that they've become so committed to active listening that sometimes when they're driving the car and the person in the right seat speaks to them, they often turn their head to try and give eye contact to the speaker, who then shouts in horror, "Will you keep your eye on the road!"

This doesn't mean the speakers like it. No, they don't, but they know there's nothing that can be done. This places a stress on the communication process, an extra obligation on the listener to apply verbal acknowledgment and appropriate facial expression as if this were a phone conversation.

But what about the choice situations? I don't have the time, or I don't want to listen?

Here's where we employ the second of our communication skills, the skill of buying time. Before we move on to learning that skill let's examine several common situations where active listening needs to be applied.

In one medical group, the administrator had a large office, wonderful furniture and a prized chair. It was large, comfortable and it swiveled. When staff came to talk with him, he'd lean back (not forward), look up at the ceiling (not at them) and swivel his chair around (which they perceived as the ultimate lack of interest). He couldn't figure out why he didn't have the cooperation of his staff.

After we worked together, examining his listening habits and teaching him the skill of active listening, he never sat in that chair when anyone was talking to him, and staff cooperation changed overnight.

Does this apply to you or anyone else at your facility?

At another group the nursing supervisor's office had a window which faced onto the facility lobby so she could see everything that was going on out there.

When patients or staff came to talk with her, her eyes could follow the path of all personnel walking by her window. She would sometimes even smile or wave to passers by, all to the frustration and consternation of anyone in her office. Is there any wonder that she faced problems of noncompliance from patients and virtual hostility from staff? They all thought that they were unimportant to her, that she was more interested in what was going on outside than in what they were saying. Yet, she told me, "I hear every word they say and I can repeat it back word for word. What do they want from me?"

No doubt you've already come up with a solution, one as simple as facing her desk another way. She chose to draw the drapes and only have them open if there was no one in the office with her.

Are there drapes, windows and office desk placements at your facility that need to be examined?

What distractions keep you from giving others 100 percent of your attention? Could it be a picture window? Could it be a gadget that keeps moving and keeps your eyes glued to it?

Could it be a letter you were reading that's still on your desk? Whatever it is, get rid of it, or arrange your office and desk so that those distractions cannot interfere with your full 100 percent active listening when someone speaks to you.

Remember...

There is no such thing as a part-time listener! When you talk to me, you own me 100 percent!

Active listening

Eye contact _____ ____ _____

Body language _____ _____

Verbal acknowledgement

_____

_____

_____

_____

Appropriate facial expression

_____

_____

CHAPTER TWO

Buying Time

"To choose time is to save time."

Francis Bacon

Okay, you're a great active listener when you can be, when time permits you to be. But what about those circumstances when you need to go to a meeting and someone wants to talk with you, or you're in the middle of preparing a report and they want to talk. Aren't your work and your needs as valid as theirs?

Absolutely, and this is when you must make a decision. Is it more important for you to focus on what you're writing than to listen to them? Is it more important for you to get to that meeting than to listen to them? Or, is it more important to listen to them?

If it's more important to listen to them, drop whatever else you are doing and listen — 100 percent active listening. Remember, there is no such thing as a part-time listener, it's either 100 percent or nothing.

Don't try to keep working while they're talking — it won't work. Don't walk down the hall while listening. That's not active and it won't work. When you decide that you must do your work first or you must go to that meeting first, use the skill of buying time.

Buying time allows you to do your work while still satisfying the other person's need to know that they are important to you and that they will get their time to speak to you. Buying time consists of four components:

1. Say their name;
2. Say something nice (preferably about them);
3. State your circumstances; and
4. Make an alternate arrangement.

STEP 1. Say their name

Our objective is to get their attention and to validate them as human beings (before we tell them we can't listen now). Nothing works as well to get another to stop and listen as hearing their name. Nothing sounds as sweet to another person as hearing their name. So say it.

STEP 2. Say something nice

Remember, we know we're about to tell them we can't listen now so we want them to feel good about themselves before we "postpone the listening." We have started to do this by saying their name. Now we say something nice about them.

Some classic comments sound like this:

"Jim, I really want to hear what you have to say ..."
"Tom, every time we talk you give me useful information ..."
"Jane, it's always a pleasure working with you ..."

You get the idea. Say something that will bring a glow to them internally.

STEP 3. State your circumstances

Now it's time to let them know what you're doing or about to do that prevents you from listening. For example:

"John, I really do want to hear about your trip to the hospital, but right now I'm in the middle of preparing this report ..."
"Jane, I always learn something when we're together, but right now I'm on my way to a director's meeting ..."

Notice that you've built up the other person's self-esteem having said their name and something nice, then, you simply related the facts. Now, move on to step number four.

STEP 4. Make an alternate arrangement

Simply suggest a time when you know you would be available to actively listen to them. In total, it might sound like this:

"John, I really do want to hear about your trip to the hospital, but right now I'm in the middle of preparing this report. I should be done by 3:30 this afternoon. Could we talk then? "

"Jane, I always learn something when we're together, but right now I'm on my way to a director's meeting. I figure that I will be done by around noon, so let me give you a call when I get out so we can talk this afternoon, maybe around 1 p.m. Is that okay?"

Yes, there are shortcuts. You probably know people who simply say, "I'm busy now, see me later." In essence they are using step 3 and step 4, stating the circumstance and making an alternate arrangement, and it is better to do that than to be a nonactive listener. But now you know an even better approach, the total four step approach of buying time.

Want to build relationships? Want to keep patients happy, staff happy? Validate them when they want to talk with you and you don't have time to listen.

Say their name. Watch a smile come to their face.

Say something nice. Watch that smile widen.

You've validated them, so now they're ready to accept your circumstances, ready to work with you on an alternate arrangement.

Buying time serves you well under other circumstances:

Interrupters

You're in a conversation with someone and another person interrupts. What do you do? Do you turn and give attention to the interrupter? Believe me, the first person won't like it. Do you ignore the interrupter? Not only won't they like it, but they'll probably keep interrupting.

You may say that they should know better and that they shouldn't interrupt. But that's not the point. They already have interrupted. You can't change their behavior since it has already manifested itself. What will you do in response? Your response is in your control.

Buy time. Call the interrupter by name, say something nice about them and tell them you're involved with someone else right now and offer an alternate arrangement.

Rambling talkers

You're in a conversation with someone and they just keep talking and talking and talking. You're a great active listener, but you now realize that you've allocated as much time to this person as you can at this moment. What do you do?

Sadly, some people begin to fidget, to look away or to look at their watch. All this serves to do is unnerve the speaker. They were so happy and content a moment ago when you were actively listening. Now you're not and they feel uncomfortable.

Just buy time. It might sound something like, "John, I'm fascinated by the details of your experience in radiology, but I just realized I must be at the pharmacy in one minute, so let's pick this up next time we meet, okay?

The telephone

The telephone is the master interrupter of all time. So innocent, it just sits there on your desk, and then, with no control by you, it keeps on ringing unless you do something about it.

"The telephone is the master interrupter of all time."

What if someone is in your office with you when the phone rings? Ideally, if you have secretarial help, that shouldn't happen, simply have the secretary handle the call.

No secretary? Use your voice mail. The person calling has no more right to your time than the person there with you. In fact, I give priority to the one I'm with.

But what if there's no secretary and no voice mail and someone is talking to me and my phone is ringing? What then? I buy time. Before I pick up the phone I might say, "Jane, I really want to hear the rest of what happened with that patient, but the phone is going to drive me crazy. Let me pick it up and see who it is."

Remember, the four steps of buying time. Don't just rush to pick up the phone. Even though the other person heard it, when you rush to pick it up they get the impression that the phone is more important than they are, and that's not the message you want to convey, is it?

Again the telephone, but this time let's imagine it got there first. The phone rings and you, the receptionist, answer it. You're talking on the phone and a patient walks into the office and stands there at the desk. What do you do? Buy time!

How? With whom?

Use hand and face signals, but don't ignore the person who just walked in.

Yes, they can see you're on the phone, but they don't want to be ignored. Sadly, some receptionists regard the patient who just walked in as an "intruder" so they turn their backs on that person and keep going with their phone conversation. And how does the patient feel?

Other receptionists who haven't been trained in buying time, ignore the patient — hoping they'll go away. Sometimes they do — forever! Try doing this:

- Even while on the phone the receptionist can smile at the patient who just walked in. That's a form of acknowledgment, almost like saying their name;
- After that welcoming smile the receptionist can wave his or hand in welcome. Yes, even while on the phone they can do that, and this represents a form of saying (doing) something nice;
- After the welcoming smile and the warm wave of the hand, the receptionist can point to the phone. That's letting the other person know what the status is; and
- After the welcoming smile, the warm wave of the hand and the pointing to the phone, the receptionist can easily hold up two or three fingers and then point to a chair. That's letting the other person know it will be another two or three minutes — please have a seat and I'll be with you then.

Yes, it is possible to buy time even when on the phone, without saying a word.

The telephone rings. A patient wants to talk with the doctor but the doctor is busy. He might be with a patient, or be in the laboratory or the lavatory, but he is not able to talk at that moment. What do you do? Buy time!

Sadly, some nurses and receptionists simply say, "The doctor is busy." But worse, they sometimes say, "The doctor is with a patient now." What's worse about that? It implies that the doctor is with someone more important than the caller. But they're his or her patient too. It is better to say, the doctor is with *another* patient. This validates the importance of both people.

The whole scenario might sound like this:

"Mr. Smith (that's his name), I'd love to put you through to Dr. Jones now (that's something nice) but he's in with another patient now (the status). As soon as he gets finished I'll give him your message."

The lurkers

You're in your office, working on some papers, or deep in thought, and someone comes to your doorway, and just stands there. He doesn't say anything, seemingly doesn't interrupt, but just stands there. Their presence can drive you crazy. What do you do? Either drop what you're doing and be an active listener or buy time. Now you have a choice and you need no longer remain at your desk, uncomfortable with the situation.

Two directions

Two patients, two employees or two colleagues both want to talk to you at the same time. What do you do? Buy time!

It's your decision who will get your attention now and who will get it later but the approach is still the same. Pick the one whom you will delay and say their name. Then say something nice about them. They see what's happening, that you're being torn, so verify it for them, and give them an approximation of when you will be with them.

What's that? You say that approach isn't perfect? Agreed. In fact, nothing in this book is perfect. We're dealing with people and they don't always act the same at all times, but this approach of buying time works most of the time with most people. But you can't shortcut the approach. It's got to be the full-fledged four component approach with attention paid to validation so that even though they're disappointed that they don't have you now, they feel good about themselves, they know you feel good about them and they'll have your full attention soon.

Remember the husband in that melodrama I lived through and described earlier in the book? The one that kept reading while his wife talked? Yes, he has rights. But, even though he doesn't want to stop reading now, he should not ignore her. Ideally, he still should put the paper down and actively listen, but if he doesn't want to, what he could have said was:

"Her name (Jane or Honey). I do want to hear about the trip, but I'm right in the middle of getting caught up on what's been happening in baseball this week. Let me finish reading it and then I'll be with you in just 15 minutes, okay?"

Can't you just see and label the four steps? They work in almost any situation.

And what about the situation where the patient is giving you information. If you look away that's bad for communication, but if you don't write it down, that's bad for therapy or might even go against policy. What do you do? The four steps of buying time:

"Mrs. Jones (her name). This is such valuable information you're giving me. I'll never remember it all. Let me write it down and then I want to hear more."

Again, the four steps are used. Mrs. Jones will appreciate both the work you're doing and the care you're giving her. When she talks, she'll feel listened to. When you write, she stops talking — but she still feels important. When you're done, you're right back to her, giving her the 100 percent active listening she craves. You gather the information you need, and Mrs. Jones is convinced she's getting the best care possible.

It isn't enough to just read about the skill. Even before you use it, you need to practice it in the seclusion of your office or home. Now is the best time to start. Think of someone who often interrupts you. What would you say to that person? Think of someone who often comes into your office while you're in the middle of doing something and just starts talking. What would you do or say? Think of someone who comes to you and says, "Do you have a few minutes?" And you just don't have the time now. What would you say? Think of a patient from whom you need information that you need to record. What would you say?

In all cases:

- say their name;
- say something nice (preferably about them);
- state your circumstances; and
- make an alternate arrangement.

Buying time

Say _____ _____

Say _____ _____

Describe _____ _____

Make _____ _____

CHAPTER THREE

Paraphrasing

"In other words...you have
no health insurance?"

"How well we communicate is determined not by how well we say things but by how well we are understood."

Andrew S. Grove, CEO, Intel Corp.
One on One with Andy Grove, G.P. Putnam's Sons, 1987

Fine. Wonderful. Let's assume we have the time to be a great active listener, and we are. We have catered to their number one need — the need to feel listened to.

Now their number two need kicks in — the need to feel understood.

Now, it's no longer enough for them to see you giving them attention, now they need and want more. They need to know that you understood what they were telling you. You don't have to agree with them, they just want to know that you understood.

"Use your own words."

There's only one way you can cater to that need and that's to paraphrase.

Loosely defined, it's letting the other person know, using your own words, what it is you understood they were saying.

It's not enough just to say, "I understand." That doesn't let them know *what* you understand, and it doesn't let them know that their message has been accurately received.

It's not enough just to repeat back what they said word for word. That proves you heard and it proves you have a good memory, but it does not prove you understand. You must use your own words to let them know what you understand.

Most paraphrases begin with words like:

- In other words ...;
- You mean that ...;
- I understand you to be saying that ...; and
- Let me see if I understand you. You're saying that ...

Now you let them know your understanding. If your paraphrase matches their transmission, wonderful. They feel listened to, they feel understood and you're sure there will be no misunderstanding. Now let them continue. Remember, we're still catering to their number two need, the need to feel understood, and the only way you can cater to that need is to listen and paraphrase. Your time to talk will come later.

Suppose your paraphrase doesn't match their transmission? Wonderful. You've given them a second chance, and they appreciate it. There would have been a misunderstanding if you hadn't paraphrased. But, you did paraphrase, and now they can say it over, say it somewhat differently and then you can paraphrase again.

Sooner or later your paraphrase will match their transmission. They'll feel understood and the both of you will have avoided a potential misunderstanding.

What should be paraphrased? Just about everything. When someone speaks, they may not hear exactly what they say, so they might not have said exactly what they wanted to. They'll never know unless you paraphrase, and then they'll hear it, be thankful and get a chance to straighten it out.

When you listen, you don't hear every word that's said. Sometimes you miss something. Sometimes you're thinking about one thing while they continue to speak. In other words, you don't catch it all.

When you paraphrase you let the other person know what you've caught. You give them a chance to fill in the missing parts, if there are any.

Doesn't this take time? Yes it does! Is it worth it? Yes it is, from two points of view:

1. The other person feels understood and that builds relationships, keeps patients coming back and keeps staff anxious to work with each other; and
2. Mistakes and misunderstandings are held to a minimum. I often wonder why we are rushed and have no time to get matters clear and straight the first time, but we have all the time in the world to straighten out a mess when things weren't understood clearly the first time.

If you believe this concept, please start paraphrasing now. Combined with your active listening, patients are going to want to be under your care and colleagues will be anxious to work with you. But if you're still not convinced and don't intend to paraphrase everything, at least paraphrase the following:

- indefinite antecedent;
- indefinite time frame; and
- indefinite modifier.

Indefinite antecedent

"Oh, how it flies into conversation." In the first sentence there is an indefinite modifier "it" which could refer to any number of nouns. Indefinite antecedents can cause many misunderstandings without the use of paraphrasing.

Suppose your colleague said to you, "They went to the meeting and Jim said it couldn't be done." Two indefinites, "they" and "it." A perfect time to paraphrase each one.

"You mean Jane and Harry went?" "Yes."

"In other words we can't change the office hours?" "No, that isn't it. We can't get assigned parking in the lot."

Notice, in the first paraphrase, your paraphrase matched the other person's transmission — perfect understanding. They felt listened to and felt understood.

In the second example, your paraphrase didn't match their transmission. No problem, because it gives them a chance to straighten you out. They feel understood and we have avoided a possible problem. If I had not paraphrased I might have told others what I believed was true — that we couldn't change the office hours — and that rumor might have spread, as fact, throughout the organization. That one paraphrase helped prevent it.

It and they — classic antecedents, which all too often are indefinite.

Couldn't a question also be used? Yes, it is possible to ask, "Who are they?" and "What is 'it' to get an answer, but I recommend the paraphrase for two reasons:

1. People don't like to be questioned. Questions make many people feel uncomfortable. In this case the paraphrase serves just as well. I'll reserve questions for those instances when no other communication device can be used; and
2. If you question, and you get an answer, you've clarified and prevented a misunderstanding, but the other person will not feel understood. People don't feel understood when they are talking, they only feel understood when you paraphrase back your understanding. Questions don't do that — paraphrases do.

Indefinite time frame

"It won't be long before paraphrasing will become part of your routine." Did you notice the indefinite time frame? "It won't be long." To some people that means one day, to others one week and I know some people who think that means one month. What did I mean?

Of course you could ask me, "How long?" You'd have the information, but I wouldn't have the verification that I had been understood. Instead, if you had said, "You mean I'll be paraphrasing routinely by tomorrow?" I might have responded, "Maybe that's a trifle quick — I think it will take about a week." We would have communicated clearly and I would be confident you understood. You were listening and I felt listened to and understood.

"Soon." That's another indefinite in time. To some people "soon" means within the hour, to others within the day and to others, weeks or months. (Would you believe that some people believe that "soon" means that the speaker really has no idea when the task will be done, so they use "soon" as a catch-all.)

When someone speaks to you and they say "soon," they know what they mean by it. You know what you would mean by it. Now it's essential to make sure that your concept of soon matches their concept and the paraphrase is the best way to check it out.

So, when someone says they'll get to me "soon" I paraphrase, "You mean by 9:15 a.m.?" But that's not the only possible paraphrase. I could have said, "In other words you'll call me in 10 minutes."

As long as you let the other person know what you're understanding, that's a good paraphrase. Whether it matches their transmission remains to be seen, but you've done your part by letting them know you've been listening and what it is you're understanding. It becomes their job to either verify or supply the correct information. In either case, you both win.

Indefinite modifier

"The project is pretty much done." How many times have you heard that or something similar? What's their idea of pretty much done? What's your idea? Do they match? Of course it's possible to ask, "Well, how much is done?" But as mentioned earlier, I prefer to paraphrase rather than question.

I know what my idea of pretty much done is so I paraphrase and say, "You mean it will be finished by tomorrow?" That's my understanding of "pretty much done." Another might paraphrase, "In other words it's 90 percent completed." Both paraphrases are perfect. They tell the speaker what the listener understands and they wait for verification.

If you don't paraphrase, your definition of "pretty much done" and the speakers definition may or may not match.

In seminar after seminar, I ask people what "pretty much done" means to them. Out of a group of a hundred, they respond by telling me that to 10 of them, it means 25 percent completed, to 50 of them between 60 percent and 75 percent completed and to the other 40 "pretty much done" means between 95 percent and 99 percent completed.

We all laugh at this exercise, realizing that within that very room there are many opportunities for problems and misunderstandings. Participants walk away convinced that they must paraphrase to avoid misunderstanding and I remind them that the even bigger benefit is that the other person will feel understood and be anxious to work and cooperate with them.

Some other examples of indefinite modifiers are:

"Close to target." How might you paraphrase that? You know you'd better paraphrase, because your idea of close to target and theirs might be miles apart. Don't ask them, tell them what you understand that to mean. That's your paraphrase. You prevent misunderstandings and enhance communication because they'll feel listened to.

"Give or take." What would your paraphrase be? Once again, you must paraphrase because you have no idea what extent they're giving or taking. What you do have is your idea of what it means to you. That's the basis of the paraphrase.

Have you ever heard one professional say to another, "Mr. Harris' hematocrit is low." If you're involved, don't let it go at that. Now you could paraphrase, "You mean it's 20?"

A companion comment might also be, "His hemoglobin is down." Don't you see how easy it would now be for you to paraphrase and say, "In other words it's at eight."

In both cases, your paraphrase might be accurate or it might not. That's not important. Both are wonderful paraphrases because they represent what you think the other person meant. Now you give the other person a chance to confirm, or to give a precise number and you're both on the same track.

Concepts

These are those simple little statements which "everyone is supposed to understand" and which are understood so differently by different people. Someone says to you about their experience with the laboratory, "Oh, you know how the lab works."

Of course you could say, "No, I don't know, how does it work?" That would get you an answer, but it sounds confrontive and that's not our goal with either patients or colleagues.

You could say, "What do you mean?" That works better, but it's still a question and people hate to be asked questions, because it still doesn't let them know that you've understood.

It's better to paraphrase:

- "You mean they're kind of slow";
- "You mean they're so busy"; or
- "In other words you're dissatisfied with the operation."

Any of those paraphrases might represent what you think they're saying. You paraphrase for understanding and to let them know you're working to understand. They feel listened to and understood. Their needs are being catered to, and unless the circumstances are so horrible, they'll keep coming back because they feel good about it all.

Have you ever had a patient say to you, "Oh, that Doctor Jones — he's impossible."

"Paraphrases are not pure guesses."

That's an example of something that's so vague, it would be a pure guess to paraphrase, and paraphrases are not pure guesses.

But rather than ask them a question like, "What do you mean?" Encourage them to talk by saying, "Tell me more." They'll hear your receptiveness and give further details. Of course you will listen actively and then, paraphrase. But now you will have an information base on which you can draw for your paraphrase. Remember, paraphrases are not guesses. They are your understanding of what's been said.

What would you say if a patient said, "I don't understand this therapy I'm on." Some might ask, "What don't you understand?" That would work, but again, it's a question. Instead, try, "You mean why you have to take the medicine for two weeks?"

This is not to say that questions are bad. We'll work with them at greater length later, but questions do not help other people feel listened to and they tend to put many people on the defensive — that is not our goal. Because we do have a wonderful alternative, the paraphrase, let's use it to clarify communications and help other people get their number two communication need filled — to feel understood.

Are you satisfied that I understand everything you want me to understand?

You mean that ...
In other words ...

Beware	**Beware**
Indefinite antecedent	it, they
Indefinite time frame	soon
Indefinite modifier	pretty much done
	close to target
	fairly clean
	give or take

I know that you believe you understand what you think I said, but I am not sure you realize that what you heard is not what I meant.

CHAPTER FOUR

"I" and "You"
Plus
"We" and "It"

"Praise loudly! Blame softly ..."

Catherine II < the Great >,
The Complete Works of Catherine II

At last, we've helped the other person feel listened to and feel understood, so they're ready and they're anxious to know what you think, to know what your plan is or what you will be doing to solve a problem. They feel so fulfilled inside they'll actually ask you to speak.

That's the perfect time to enter the conversation — by invitation.

But what do you say ... and how do you say it?

Basically, we can speak in four dimensions:

1. "I" — ourselves. This "I" also applies to the group and the entity and the hospital. It includes you, the staff and others, but it does not include the person to whom you are speaking;
2. "You" — the person to whom you are speaking;
3. "We" (be careful about this). In the context of communication, "we" means the speaker and the listener. Yes, it does include the listener. Therefore, the comment, "we at the Jones Medical Group believe ..." Is not a "we" statement. It's really a pluralization or extension of "I." Remember, if it doesn't include the listener, it's not a we statement, even if the word "we" is used in the statement; and
4. "It" refers to the activity, the event, the X-ray or the schedule. It even refers to another person not participating in the conversation. Thus "he" is really in the "it" category for purposes of communication.

What we say, how we say it and how we focus our sentences will affect our communication. Let's first recognize that people focus very closely on the first words of any sentence — the first words of what appear to be a cohesive thought. Sometimes they drift off, but they hear and react to those first words.

The words "you" or saying their name are the most powerful opening words you can use. They always get the other person to tune in. In fact, they almost put the other person into a fight/flight position. When anyone talks about them, they're ready to defend.

Thus the first rule of speaking to others: when you use the word "you" or use their name, follow it with some favorable or complimentary remark. They will hear the word "you," get ready to defend and then relax when they hear the favorable remark. Put another way, start sentences with the word "you" when you're going to compliment.

Sentences which begin with the word "I" allow the speaker to enter a topic without alarming the listener. As long as you're talking about yourself, your group, your organization or your staff, the listener will be less interested than if you were talking about him or her, but they won't feel threatened.

Thus the second rule of speaking to others: When you use the word "I" (individual or collective), it's okay to lead into topics that might be controversial, even adversarial. The adrenaline is not flowing. Some people advocate, use "I" to take responsibility and "you" to compliment and give credit.

> "Use 'I' to take responsibility and 'you' to give credit."

Sentences which begin with the word "we" are inclusive, coupling and team building sentences, provided they include the listener as an equal, as a partner and not as appendage.

Sentences which begin with the word "it" either as a thing or "third person she, he, they" are neutral in nature and help focus on the event, the circumstance or the activity. Use "it" to focus away from the speaker and the listener.

Now let's put the theory into practical, daily use.

Suppose a patient who is habitually late comes to the office on time. When you talk to the patient you have your choice of how to speak. You could:

1. Focus on yourself and say, "I'm certainly glad I gave you that card and called you to remind you about the appointment." Hardly a way to win friends, but sadly, there are people who do "hog the credit" and focus on themselves.
2. Focus on "it" by saying, "This appointment will be filled right on schedule." Businesslike, very business like. No harm done, but no good done either, and what a lost opportunity to work on building a relationship.
3. Focus on "we" by saying, "We certainly work great together — you're right on time and I'll get you right in." A big step forward. Two people get credit, both sharing in an achievement. A winner.
4. Focus on the patient by saying, "Mr. Jones, you're right on time. Thank you for your promptness. You really help the office operate most efficiently.

We recommend both number three and number four to our clients. Be generous with praise. Start the sentence with "you," add the compliment and you build relationships with patients. Start the sentence with "we" and build a team. In both cases the patient will come back again and again.

What about some less pleasant circumstances? Let's say the patient is late? Now what?

Admittedly this is not as easy, and certainly not as much fun as the earlier scenario, but one that has to be faced up to.

It's no longer a case of how much we can build, but it's now a case of how we face reality, without driving a patient away.

Again, there are four choices:

1. We could focus on "you" and say, "You're late Mr. Jones, and that's not good. You're just going to have make your plans more accurately in the future."
2. We could focus on "we" and say, "We have a problem Mr. Jones. I need to fulfill Doctor Smith's schedule and you want to get your 3:30 time slot, even though you were late." Let's see what we can do about it.
3. We could focus on "I" and say, "I have a problem Mr. Jones. I had a spot reserved for you at 3:30, but I had to fill it when I didn't see you. I'll do my best to squeeze you later this afternoon, but I can't guarantee any specific time. I wish I could do better than that, but I can't."
4. We could focus on "it" and say, "This appointment book was screaming at 3:30, some 15 minutes ago. It had an opening for you Mr. Jones, but it couldn't find you, so the appointment had to be given away. Let's see what it can arrange for later today."

"Sadly, there are some personnel who take great delight in "scolding" a patient."

Sadly, there are some personnel who take great delight in "scolding" a patient. They use communication approach number one, the worst communication choice possible. There's something to be said about options number two, number three and number four — they all protect the patient, which is good.

Option number two involves the speaker so the patient is not alone, even though there's a powerful "you" blaming statement within. That statement, even though it's within the sentence and even though it's covered by "we" could still anger the patient.

Option number three almost makes it appear that the responsibility lies with the speaker. Hard to swallow? Perhaps, but it tends to insulate the patient and we certainly want the patient to feel accepted. They generally know they're late and they don't need a scolding. They don't need blame dumped on them. This option even has the speaker being apologetic for not being able to get the patient in immediately and patients like that kind of treatment.

Option number four. Who can get mad at an appointment book? Certainly not Mr. Jones, when he knows he missed the time. And beside, the appointment book will work at arranging an alternate.

It almost comes down to personal preference. Which approach would you be most comfortable with?

Let's rule out number one. Let's accept that number two is acceptable, but not the best. Think about number three and number four. Are you courageous enough to shoulder some responsibility, even though you weren't the person who was late? If you can, most patients prefer that kind of treatment, but if that's not your personal style, try number four. Focus on the book, but avoid those damaging "you" statements at all costs.

Compliments? — Always start with "you."

Compliments do not apply to patients alone. They apply equally to colleagues or employees. When things go right, heap praise. Start sentences with "you." Give them the credit. When things don't go right, avoid "you" statements. They bring out defenses, resentment and hostility. Instead, use any of the other three options to build a team, to take the blame yourself or to focus on a time clock and schedule.

Patient, colleague or employee; they all have their pride and ego. Build it when circumstances allow it, nurture it at every opportunity and preserve it when circumstances might be buffeting it and you'll build relationships that will benefit you personally and the organization as well.

What about less specific situations, but ones that come up every day. Suppose the patient needs to go to X-ray. How could you direct the patient?

- "You" focuses by saying, "You've got to go to X-ray now." This may be true from the perspective of the organization, but not necessarily from the patient's point of view. Nobody likes to be told what they have to do;
- "I" focuses by saying, "I need an X-ray to allow me to see if it's a break or not. I'll set it up with the technician." Easy enough for the patient to understand and easy enough for their ego to swallow;
- "We" focuses by saying, "We need an X-ray so that we can work together on the best way to treat this"; and
- "It" focuses by saying, "the diagnosis won't be complete without an X-ray. The technician will handle all the details."

In another common scenario, a patient asks you how to get to the GI Lab and you know it's in an out of the way location. Ideally, you or someone else would take the patient there, but let us say that's not possible today.

- "You" focuses by saying, "You're liable to have some troubles finding it. You've got to be very careful. You must avoid — and you must ...";
- "I" focuses by saying, "I wish I could take you there but I can't. I always have a hard time finding it myself, but I've worked out a system. First I go down the hall, then I ... I'm sure that if I can find it you'll surely be able to find it too";
- "We" focuses by saying, "We've got our work cut out for us on this one. I'll do my best to explain and we'll need your closest attention to the details"; or
- "It" focuses by saying, "The GI Lab isn't far away, but it isn't easy to find. It sits on the lower level behind the employee lounge. It's easiest to find by going down the rear steps to ..."

Compliments and complaints

How would you handle a compliment given to you by a patient? Of course, the simplest way is to say "Thank you." In fact, thank you are two words that should be used quite liberally. Whenever someone tells you anything, be it a compliment or some other information, the first words that you should say are "Thank you" or "Thank you for telling me."

Doesn't that get trite? Not to the other person. People enjoy being thanked, especially when they believe they've done something worthwhile.

When they give you a compliment, they think its worthwhile and they find nothing trite about a thank you to them for something they have done.

When they give you some information, they think it's worthwhile and so they find nothing trite about a thank you to them for information they have given.

When they complain, they think that's worthwhile, and that some corrective action will be taken, so they find nothing trite about a thank you.

It's from their perspective and, after all, if we're to satisfy our "customers," it's their perspective that's important.

But from our perspective, the thank you is equally appropriate. After all, don't you like to hear a compliment? Aren't you thankful? Then why not say it and let them feel good too?

Furthermore, when someone gives you information, isn't that helpful? If you didn't know what they told you then you've learned something and you're now in a position to do something. Wouldn't you be thankful for that? Then tell them!

Even if they complain to you — whatever it is they're complaining about is valid from their perspective. By listening, you extend an acceptance that they need. And when they're done, if they've given you valuable information, "thank you" is certainly in place.

Even if you believe that their complaint has no basis and you learned nothing new, you should be thankful they told you. Because you were there for them to complain to and for them to ventilate to, they'll feel better. They'll be less likely to complain to other patients or friends about their unhappiness and be more likely to remain with your group.

> Compliment or complaint, your first words should be, "Thank you for telling me."

Let's complete our scenario of compliments and complaints.

How would you handle a compliment given to you by a patient? Of course, the simplest way is to say, "Thank you." But some patients like to hear more and some people, maybe you, like to say more. Your choices are:

- "You" focuses by saying, "Thank you. You're very kind Ms. Smith." A winner!;
- "I" focuses by saying. "Thank you. I deserve it. I work very hard around here." A loser!;
- "It" focuses by saying, "Thank you. The clinic appreciates it. It's not just me, it's everyone working here that makes it all happen." Acceptable; or
- "We" focuses by saying, "Thank you. We both deserve the compliment. You do your share by spreading your good will and I love to hear it. You and I make a great team." A winner!

And, if a complaint comes your way again, there are four choices.

- "I" focuses by saying, "Thank you for telling me. I'll certainly look into it." A winner!;
- "We" focuses by saying, "Thank you for telling me. We'll both benefit from your comments." Another winner!;
- "It" focuses by saying, "Thank you for telling me. Information of this nature is very helpful." Acceptable; or
- "You" focuses by saying, "Thank you for telling me, but you really don't know all of the details of the hard work that goes on around here. Maybe if you spent as many hours here as others do you wouldn't complain like that." Don't even think about it!

Remember, the more someone complains to me, the more thankful I am. And I'm very serious when I say to them, "Thank you for telling me."

Obviously we're not going to cover every possible set of circumstances in detail, but be aware that you have a choice of words and you have a choice of focus. Ask yourself, how shall I start my part of the conversation? The very first words are key. Will they be "I," "you," "we" or "it" focused? Do I have a chance to say thank you?

The time spent considering the focus and the choice of words will be more than worth it as you start new relationships, preserve relationships and build relationships.

I

accept responsibility,

You

give praise

CHAPTER FIVE

The Reversal

"Thank you, doctors! I guess I didn't
express myself clearly!"

"Make the communication process a circle. To measure the receiver's understanding, ask for feedback in the form of a paraphrased statement. If the statement does not coincide with your meaning, patiently restate your message."

Elaine Estervig Beaubien, Edgewood College, Madison, WI, writing in Tidbits, Tips and Tales

Congratulations! You're a great communicator and everyone likes to talk to you, be with you and confide in you. When they speak, they feel listened to because you're a great active listener. When they speak they feel understood because you're a great paraphraser. And when you can't give them a full 100 percent attention at the moment, they're still okay because you've become proficient as a buyer of time.

When you get to speak, they love it too because you choose your focus carefully. When there's credit to be given they get a share of the credit. When there's a problem, you share in the responsibility and when there are other items to be discussed, the focus stays on the items, not the individuals.

"Wonderful. But what about me? Who caters to me when I'm the speaker?

"Or what about when I talk to my boss and he just leans back in his chair and looks up at the ceiling. I feel lousy. How do I get him to be an active listener?

"Or when I talk to a colleague and she keeps looking around the room, out the window, down the hall — but rarely at me. It's frustrating, but what can I do about it — she's really a nice person and besides, she doesn't work for me.

"Even if she does work for me, what can I do, force her to look at me? I can't. I've got several employees who just look down at the floor when I talk to them. I can't "order" them to look at me, can I?"

And so it goes, questions from people asking what to do when others aren't active listeners.

I can't say the solution is easy because it's never as easy to change the behavior of others as it is to change our own behavior. First, let's recognize the options that are open:

Ignore it

Your body will feel the effects, but it's an option. After meeting with this person, find another person who is a good active listener and speak to them and you can get those good feelings that you must have missed in the previous conversation. In fact, certain situations force non-active listening. Staff in the operating room must communicate, yet they can't be giving each other eye contact, etc. After surgery, each member should find someone who can give them the active listening that they've been lacking for the past hour or more.

Another situation is during any joint activity, for instance when both parties are focused on a subject, like an X-ray or a report, yet they are talking to each other. Neither may be able to listen actively to the other because of the work that needs to be done. After it's over, find another person who is a good active listener and speak to them so that you can get those good feelings that you missed in the previous conversation. Therefore, if it's your boss who's not listening actively and you're not comfortable using any of the other options we'll offer — ignore it. If it's a colleague and you're not comfortable using any of the other options given — ignore it. If it's a patient, the best option is probably to ignore it. That's part of the price of the job.

Stop talking

Generally speaking, when a listener isn't giving eye contact, they're still "hearing," and when they hear a silence instead of a sound, they'll turn to the speaker to see what's happening. Once you've got their eyes again, start talking and maybe they'll stay with you longer this time.

Ask a question

Obviously, when you ask a question you get the listener involved. In fact, they've become the speaker. The drawback is you are no longer the speaker and you no longer get your chance to express your views. You're not getting the good feeling of being listened to and being understood. So, after they've expressed their answer to your question, regain the floor, and maybe, this time, since you've 'involved' them they'll stay with you longer.

Speak louder

Just as listeners react to silence they react to a change in decibels. Raise your voice — they'll look at you. Speak softer. They'll react the same as if you spoke louder. In fact, this combination is what many people use with listeners who don't seem to be actively listening. They raise their voice, they lower their voice and they sometimes go silent, but at least they've still got the floor.

Face the issue

If you've been a great active listener yourself, you've set a wonderful example and if the person involved is someone you have regular conversations with, face the issue. How? Say to the other person, "Jim, I need to check something with you. When you were talking I did my best to look at you, stay in touch with you verbally, connect with you by leaning closer to you, and I want to check, did you feel listened to when you were talking?" Ideally, Jim will say yes. Then continue, "Well then Jim, I need the same reinforcement from you when I'm speaking. I need to see you, so please look at me rather than out the window. I need to know that you're connected to me, so please move closer instead of being so far away. Can you do that? I'd feel so much better!"

I wish I could guarantee that every time you did this the other person would respond, "Sure" and then manifest all of the skills that you've learned. But, there's a good chance that this person will try and you could be on the road to being their mentor. They'll appreciate it and you'll gain every time you're talking to them.

At last, you're a great communicator. Others feel good when they talk to you, and you feel listened to when you talk to others. It's wonderful, except, even though others look at you when you're speaking and they give you their full 100 percent attention; and even though they utter sounds, lean forward and exhibit appropriate facial expressions — they don't paraphrase. They just sit there saying, "Uh huh ... Oh ... I see ... I understand." But you have no idea of what they understand. How do you get them to paraphrase you? That requires the skill of reverse paraphrasing, sometimes called request paraphrasing.

You could ask them, "Do you understand?" But sadly, they might say "yes," and now you're almost in worse shape than you were before. Because they've said they understand, any further questioning by you might lead them to believe that you don't believe them. So don't ask, "Do you understand?" It rarely gets the desired results. Don't ask the patient, "Do you understand?" It doesn't work. Don't ask your employee, "Do you understand?" They might be afraid to say no, so they'll say yes and try and figure it out later. They might get it wrong and that's when big trouble sets in. Some people ask, "What do you think about what I just said?" But instead of getting a paraphrase of their understanding, they get opinions about the validity, acceptability and practicality of the ideas, without a basic agreement that they understood what was just said.

Don't ask them for their opinion of what was just said until they have first let you know that they understand.

Some people simply ask the other person, "Tell me what I just told you." It works, when you've got the authority, but it doesn't leave a good taste in the other person's mouth. They don't like being bossed around and they don't like the idea that you think they don't understand. And certainly, this approach couldn't be used on a colleague, a supervisor or a patient.

Is there any hope? Is there any way to get another person to paraphrase without offending them? Yes!

It's a magnificent skill that centers on another application of the use of "I" and "you" — "I" to take responsibility and "you" to give credit.

Let's assume you've been talking for a while, getting great active listening from the other person, but no paraphrasing. You're really not sure if there's complete understanding and it's important that they understand, whether it be a set of instructions for an employee, a therapeutic regimen for a patient or simply some ideas expressed to your supervisor and/or colleague. Stop for a moment and take the responsibility for the communication when you ask for the paraphrase. My favorite is, "Jane, I've been talking for a while and I'm not sure I've really said everything the way I want to say it. Please help me. What have I said so far?"

Please notice that "I'm" taking the responsibility. *I'm* taking responsibility, because *I'm* not sure *I've* done what *I* wanted to do.

Some other good examples are:

- "I've been talking for a while and I'm not sure I've covered the important points I need to cover. Tell me, what have I covered so far?";
- "This project is very important to me and I want to make sure I haven't left out any of the important points. What points have I made so far?"; and
- "You know I'm so excited about this I worry that I might have overlooked something that needs to be said. Help me. What have I said so far?"

There are many, many others, but you get the idea. The speaker takes the responsibility and the listener has no doubt, blame or implication of blame put on them — just a request to help.

This approach only works if you are ready to use it. So take a moment to write the approach you would use to get another person to paraphrase you.

Did it focus on "I"? Wonderful.

Now we recognize that two possibilities exist:

1. Their paraphrase matched our transmission; and
2. Their paraphrase did not match our transmission.

A match

Easiest one first. Let's imagine that their paraphrase *did* match our transmission. Wonderful. How fortunate you are. You've got someone who is an active listener and also understands you — and what's more, you know you've been understood, so you feel understood and that's a good feeling.

So thank your listener because you really are thankful. Here's the ideal time for a "you" statement, like: "Thanks, Jim, you sure are a great listener," or "Thanks Harriet, you certainly are a pleasure to work with." Notice the thank you. Notice they get full credit.

Then, continue on with whatever it is you were saying, secure in the knowledge they understood the first part. If they don't voluntarily paraphrase you in a while, repeat the entire process. Remember all the rules of paraphrasing that applied to you. The necessities that applied to you, apply to the other person as well. There cannot be complete communication unless the speaker speaks and the listener then paraphrases to confirm understanding.

"Doesn't this take a lot of extra time?"

Yes, it does, but consider the alternative. The alternative is risk. Maybe they did understand, and a few moments of time would have been saved. But, the risk is that there is not complete understanding and there we have the basis for misunderstanding. I will never understand why people don't have enough time to make sure things are understood the first time, but then have all the extra hours needed to correct a mistake when there's been a misunderstanding.

Finally, from a selfish point of view, it feels great to be speaking to someone, to feel listened to and then to feel understood. Remember, they are the number one and number two needs of communication that others have. But, you have them too. So, either the other person paraphrases you voluntarily, or now you know how to request one.

Okay, that was easy. You spoke, asked for a paraphrase, got one and it matched. But what if the paraphrase the listener gives doesn't match your transmission? What then?

"Thank you" are still the first words I utter.

"Are you kidding?" I've been asked by seminar attendees, "You actually say 'thank you' to someone who has just paraphrased you and they didn't understand the message?"

Right, I say, "Thank you," and quite frankly, I'm more thankful now than I was before. You see, when there was a match if I had not gotten the paraphrase, nothing bad would have happened because it turned out they understood. But in this case, they didn't understand and a problem could have resulted. So I am truly thankful that we discovered this. So, I thank them and then I continue. Please note that when I continue, I shift the focus. Before when there was a match, the focus went to them. They got all the credit. This time, when there is no match, "I" will take the responsibility. Maybe I didn't say it right, maybe I left something out, maybe I covered too much. So, I say, "Thank you, Mike, I guess I didn't say what I meant to say."

Others may choose to say something similar to, "Thank you Mary. I guess I didn't express myself clearly."

Continuing, we add, "What I meant to say is ..." Obviously we must restate whatever we said before, but we already know that the way we said it didn't work last time, so we've got to make a change. Sadly, many people just repeat exactly what they said the last time, adopting the philosophy that all that is needed is another dose of the same communication medicine. It doesn't work. Repeating the same thing the same way doesn't work.

"Repeating the same thing the same way doesn't work."

Others choose to raise their voice. They figure that the only reason there was a communication breakdown the first time is that the other person is hard of hearing, so they compensate and yell. If the other person is hard of hearing, a louder voice will work, but if they misunderstood for any other reason, yelling won't work either.

What does work?

- Say it again but in a different order. Maybe the other person had a problem making a connection. Putting it in a different order sometimes helps clarify;
- Say it again, but cover less ground. Again, there was a communication problem last time. Maybe that's because you covered too much ground. Sure, you know the subject, but they don't. You take it for granted, but they are having difficulty putting it all together, so cover less ground; and
- Say something different and come back to this later. Perhaps the extra information you give will help put the misunderstood material into perspective. Then ... it's time to ask for a paraphrase again.

"What? How long will this go on?"

As long as it's necessary to get a paraphrase that matches the transmission.

Just because you say it a second time doesn't mean there's a guarantee that they understand. It absolutely still calls for the paraphrase. Besides, don't you want to feel understood? You haven't had that feeling yet, even though you may have felt listened to.

So, how should we now ask for this paraphrase?

For me that's easy. Since I've taken responsibility for miscommunication the first time, it's easy for me to build on that and say, "Let's see if I did any better this time. Jim, what's your understanding of what I'm saying?" Notice, I continue to take responsibility.

If that doesn't sound like you, try using one of the original type requests for a paraphrase now. But remember, when you're requesting a paraphrase, be it the first time or the second time, use "I" statements. Take the responsibility.

Again we recognize that two possibilities exist:

1. Their paraphrase matched our transmission; or
2. Their paraphrase did not match our transmission.

A match

Thank your listener, because you really are thankful, and again here's the ideal time for a "you" statement like:

"Thanks, Jim, you sure are a great listener," or "Thanks, Harriet, you certainly are a pleasure to work with," or "Thanks, John, you sure stayed with it and made it work." Notice the "Thank you," notice they get full credit.

No match

This is tough. For the second time you've transmitted and the requested paraphrase didn't match your transmissions. There have been times when this has happened to me when I felt like throwing up my hands in disgust. There were times I felt like saying, "What's wrong with you?" but I didn't.

Blame doesn't work. Blame doesn't build teamwork or relationships. Blame doesn't get the patient to come back. And blame certainly doesn't get you to feel understood. Besides what gives me the right to blame the other person? Maybe I didn't say it right. Maybe I'm the one who is mixing up the ideas. Maybe it's my fault.

So, as you might have expected, the first two words I recommend you say are "Thank you!" Strange as this may sound, I'm more thankful now than ever. It's for sure my listener and I are not on the same wavelength and I'm thankful I've discovered it.

After "Thank you" I continue by taking the responsibility and add, "I don't seem to be communicating too well today," or "I don't know what's wrong with me. I guess I'm not saying exactly what I mean to say." Please notice the continued application of the rule of "I" and "you."

Some people ask, "Won't you lose face by taking so much responsibility?" Of course that's always a possibility, but not a probability. People appreciate others who are willing to let the "buck stop with them." People appreciate others who seem to take the burden and quite often will offer to share the burden by saying, "No, I think it's my fault, I may not be concentrating very well today."

> "People appreciate other people who are willing to have the 'buck' stop with them."

We're not interested in fixing blame. We need to make sure there's understanding and we still need to feel understood.

What options are open to me? The same ones that were open before, but now I must be even more careful, take even smaller bites, move even slower and search for that arena which appears to be best understood and move out from there.

Sometimes I realize a potential futility and will ask someone else to try. Maybe their way will be better than mine. Sometimes I suggest we stop and try again later, or tomorrow. Sometimes I'll put it into writing and sometimes I'll just keep plugging away until we succeed.

But every time I finish explaining, I again ask for the paraphrase. Of course by now I don't need formalities, the other person knows what is needed, so when I'm done explaining something I can simply say, "Okay, let's see how I did this time," and they'll paraphrase.

As always, when the paraphrase is right, they get all the credit. If it isn't, I'll take the responsibility.

"Communication is like a flow chart," comment my engineering friends. Indeed it is. And now we've incorporated the concept of the reverse or request paraphrase into this flow chart.

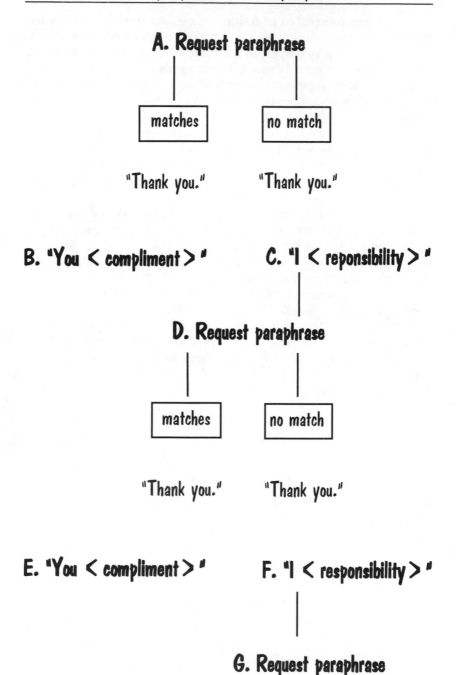

A. Request paraphrase

matches | no match

"Thank you." | "Thank you."

B. "You < compliment > "   C. "I < reponsibility > "

D. Request paraphrase

matches | no match

"Thank you." | "Thank you."

E. "You < compliment > "   F. "I < responsibility > "

G. Request paraphrase

CHAPTER SIX

Feelings

"When dealing with people, remember you are not dealing with creatures of logic, but with creatures of emotion."

Dale Carnegie

Earlier, we defined communications as being a two way exchange of facts, ideas and feelings. Up until now we've been working with facts and ideas. It's time we expanded and include the third dimension — feelings.

Dictionaries define feelings in many ways. Even the smallest pocket dictionary has at least three definitions and I've even seen one with 16 different definitions and variations.

For our purpose, let's say: a feeling is an emotion; it's something within us; it's ours and we own it; and it's neither right nor wrong — it just is.

I have a right to my feelings. I can choose to share them with you or keep them to myself, but here's the problem. When I choose to keep my feelings to myself it has an effect on me. For me, when I keep my feelings to myself, my blood pressure goes up. Other people get palpitations. Still others develop a rash, or an itch or turn red, but, feelings held in have their effect on us. That's one of the major reasons to express our feelings.

As soon as I tell you my feeling, not only have I given you the full flavor of what's happening with me, not only am I communicating more fully with you, but I am also relieving myself of the stress of holding those feelings in. So the recommendation here is, where practical, express your feelings.

Most people think they do, but they've been fooled by our language. So many people say, "I feel that this clinic does a good job." Yes, they've used the word feel, but they've expressed a thought.

"When you tell me a feeling, there is no agreement possible, no disagreement possible and no variations are possible."

"What's the difference? Who cares?" There is a difference. I care, and I hope you will too.

When you express a thought or an idea, I respect it. I thank you for being willing to tell me about it, but I reserve the right to agree with your idea, disagree with your idea or offer variations of your idea. When you tell me a feeling, there is no agreement possible, no disagreement possible and no variations are possible. It's your feeling. You own it. The best thing I can do is listen and be thankful that you were willing to share it with me.

I do recognize that there are different levels of communicating, and when you share a feeling you're reaching to the deepest level of communication.

Level one — You tell me a superficial, impersonal thought. Example: "I think it will rain today," or "Nice weather." Please notice that both are impersonal and not talking about me or yourself. On a scale of importance, the weather and rain usually rank low.

Level two — You tell me a significant impersonal thought. Example: "I think the Russian leader is making a mistake by not dealing with his political rival." Please notice, the comment is impersonal. But the significance as to how it affects the world is much higher.

Level three — You tell me a superficial personal thought. Example: "I think I'll go to the movies later this week." Notice the difference. Instead of talking about the weather or another person, you're now talking about yourself. That's personal, but the depth of revelation is superficial — movies later this week.

Level four — You tell me a significant personal thought. Example: "I think I'll retire at the end of this year" or "I think I'll change my will." Notice, it's personal — very personal — and highly significant. A deep sharing, but not the ultimate.

Level five — The ultimate sharing: you tell me a feeling. Example: "I'm worried about my future" or "I'm excited about my future." Now you're sharing from among your emotions — worry and excitement.

"So when you share a feeling the best thing I can do is listen (actively of course) and then thank you for telling me." I can't agree — there's nothing to agree with. It's your feeling and you're entitled to it. And I can't disagree for the same reasons. I can't even have variations, I can't vary your feeling.

I can have my own feelings about retirement. I can have my own feelings about my future. But right now, the best thing I can do for you is just listen, thank you for having enough confidence in me to tell your feelings and even ask you to "tell me more" if you want to.

Now that we understand the importance of feelings and their position in the hierarchy of levels of communication, let's revisit an earlier comment:

When you express a thought or an idea, I respect it. I thank you for being willing to tell me about it, but I reserve the right to agree with your idea, disagree with your idea or offer variations of your idea. When you tell me a feeling there is no agreement possible and no disagreement possible, no variations possible. It's your feeling. You own it. The best thing I can do is listen and be thankful that you were willing

to share it with me. Therefore, it becomes absolutely necessary that we recognize the difference between an expression of
a thought and the expression a feeling.

Remember our earlier example? So many people say, "I
feel that this clinic does a good job." Yes, they've used the
word feel, but they've expressed a thought. How can we tell
the difference?

The "key" lies in the word feel and the word "am." If an
expression uses the word "feel" and we can substitute the
word "am" for "feel," then that expression is a feeling. If a
expression uses the word "am" and we can substitute the
word "feel" for "am," then that expression is a feeling. But if
the substitution can't be made, it's probably not a feeling but
a thought.

Let's look at a couple of examples:

"I feel excited." Substitute "am" and it becomes "I am
excited." Yes, that makes sense. That's a logical sentence. It
must be a true feeling expression."

Another. "I feel angry." Substitute "am" and it becomes "I
am angry. Yes, that makes sense. That's a logical sentence. It
must be a true feeling expression."

Still another. "I feel troubled." Substitute "am" and it
becomes "I am troubled." Yes, that makes sense. That's a
logical sentence. It must be a true feeling expression.

Contrast those with this one. "I feel that we're on the right
track." Substitute "am" it becomes "I am that we're on the
right track." It makes no sense. That's not a logical sentence.
It must not be a true expression of a feeling. It's really a
thought and the sentence more appropriately should be, "I
think that we're on the right track."

Finally, "I feel that our patients get great treatment here."
Substitute "am" and it becomes "I am that our patients get
great treatment here." It makes no sense so it must not be a
true expression of a feeling. It's an idea. The sentence more
appropriately should be, "I think that our patients get great
treatment here."

To repeat, thoughts or ideas are not bad or unimportant,
but when you tell me an idea I reserve the right to listen, to
agree, disagree or have other perspectives on the same idea.
But when you tell me a feeling, that's different.

There's another way to double check whether you or
anyone else is expressing an idea or a feeling. The key word in
this checkup is "that."

If the word "that" is used immediately after the word "feel,"
chances are it isn't an expression of a feeling, it's a thought.

"I feel that you're right" is an acceptable sentence, but does not express a feeling. In reality it's saying, "I think" that you're right," and that's a thought.

Another example. "I feel" that America is a wonderful country. "I agree," but still it wasn't a feeling that was expressed, it was a thought. That gives me the right to agree with your thought.

The two feeling vs. thought checkups are:

1. Do the am/feel substitution check, substituting "am" for "feel"; and

2. Check for "that" immediately following "feel."

You're now in a perfect position to check your communication level. Is it Level 1, 2, 3 or 4 (all thoughts), or is it the deepest, Level 5 — feelings?

When you do choose to express your feelings you have such a wide variety of words to choose from. Our language is rich in its selection of words to express feelings from the lowest low to the highest high. A small sampling follows:

abandoned	confused
adequate	conspicuous
affectionate	contented
ambivalent	contrite
annoyed	cruel
anxious	crushed
astounded	deceitful
awed	defeated
beautiful	delighted
betrayed	desirous
bitter	destructive
bold	determined
bored	different
brave	disgusted
burdened	disturbed
calm	dominated
capable	eager
challenged	ecstatic
charmed	empty
cheated	enchanted
cheerful	energetic
childish	envious
clever	evil
competitive	exasperated
condemned	excited
	exhausted

That's 52 words and we're only up to the "Es." There are many feeling words we've even left out within the letters given. So, take a moment now to circle those feelings given that you recognize you've had within the last week and then add as many others as you can think between "exhausted" and the last one on my personal list, which is "zany."

Now that I've stated, and restated, that the way to express a feeling is to say "am" or "feel" and follow it with the word that describes the feeling, allow me to alert you that there is an exception.

Children make maximum use of this exception. They have to. They haven't learned any of the fancy words listed earlier yet, beyond tears, they need to express their feelings so they use similes.

They haven't learned how to say, "I feel insignificant" so they say something like "I feel like a little fish in a big pond." Please note, there are very few people who would not recognize the significance of that expression. Another child might express a feeling through simile by saying, "I feel like I'm a little ant and you're squashing me." Wow, powerful stuff.

As children grow up, and even as adults, they/we often use similes. Have you ever said:

- "I feel like I'm on cloud 9";
- "I feel like a bull in a china shop"; or
- "I feel like I'm sitting on top of the world."

What other similes do you use to express feelings? What similes have you heard other people use?

If, and when, you use similes to express your feelings you won't be alone and you won't necessarily be among children either. You'll be among the literate elite, the master writers through the ages who have used similes to convey the essence, the background and the flavor of their writings.

"I don't know" say some. "Admittedly, there are lots of feeling words to choose from, and I can use similes to express feelings. But I don't know if I want to express my feelings and let others know about them. Besides, what's the use, it doesn't accomplish anything anyhow."

But it does!

First, if you want to communicate and communicate fully, you need to express your ideas, your facts and your feelings. It's a partial communication if you leave out the feelings.

Second, to ignore feelings is like ignoring a warning light that indicates that an electrical circuit is overloaded. If you don't express the feeling, if you hold it back and squelch it, your body will pay a price. Evidence is emerging that squelched feelings lead to stress, to elevated blood pressure and in some cases it may even lead to a shortened life.

Yes, it's possible that when you express your feelings you do something to help yourself live longer and better.

Ideally, expressing feelings should be done with someone who is involved with that feeling, the person with whom you feel angry, the person about whom you feel proud. If that isn't possible, find another person to whom you can talk and express feelings without being interrupted, without being chastised and without being advised. And if that isn't possible, talk to yourself — out loud. Yes, it has to be out loud, those feelings need to be verbalized.

Yes, I've sometimes said to myself, "Boy Jacob, I'm angry. I'm upset. I'm frustrated. I worked so hard to arrange a schedule and the staff has changed it all and I'm left to deal with the patients. I feel like I could burst." (Catch the simile?)

"Have you ever screamed at someone, though their actions didn't warrant it?"

It would be best if I could tell it directly to the staff. But if that weren't possible, it would be better if I could tell it to a colleague, a friend or a spouse. But if even that wasn't possible, I've always got me and I can tell it to myself. And I'll continue talking until I'm satisfied that I've recognized it, said it and "feel" ready to move on. Sure beats breaking walls, kicking doors or screaming at innocent patients who wouldn't understand the frustration.

That's another consequence of the non-expression of feelings. The feelings stay squelched for a while, but they emerge, they erupt, another time, another place, often out of context, to the detriment of another person, generally innocent. Have you ever screamed at someone, though their actions didn't warrant it? I have. I was really screaming at another person in absentia. How sad.

Have you ever over-rewarded someone for an activity that didn't warrant the heightened reward? I have. I've given outlandish tips to workers, not because their service had been so spectacular, but because I was so happy about another event. I hadn't really had a chance to tell anyone about it, so I was sharing my pleasure with the attendant, the food server or the cab driver instead. They had no idea what was going on.

Finally, do you want the most logical reason for telling others your feeling? Here it is! If you don't tell them they'll guess at your feeling and they may guess wrong. Whatever it is they guess that you're feeling they'll believe they're right, and no matter what you're really feeling they will have assigned your feeling to you. So, you might as well tell them so they'll know it accurately rather than by them guessing, accurately or not.

People react so differently to different circumstances. For example, they may whistle when they feel confident and you may whistle when you feel unsure. If they hear you whistling without you adding that you're feeling unsure, they'll just transfer how they feel when they whistle and be convinced that you're feeling confident, when in reality it's just the opposite. Yes, not only do people guess what you're feeling, but the criteria they use are their own reactions, and your reactions may not match theirs. If you say nothing and let them guess they may assign a feeling to you that really isn't yours, but they'll believe it is. That's why it's so much better to just tell them.

It's better to tell the patient, "I'm so happy that the X-ray turned out negative," rather than just "The X-ray turned out negative." Better to say, "I'm disappointed that the test results haven't come back yet," rather than just say, "The test results haven't come back yet." And yes, it is better to say, "I'm sad that the regimen hasn't had the desired affect," rather than just say, "The regimen hasn't had the desired affect."

When you express your feelings, the other person gets the entire flavor of the communication and you get the benefit of having relieved your body of stress. The communication is clear. Nobody had to guess.

Still have doubts that others guess? Still have doubts that others might have different feelings about similar situations? That's not unusual. Asking "How do you feel on the last day of your vacation?" gets many different responses. Many people feel sad. They wish they could vacation longer. Some people feel angry, angry with themselves that they didn't accomplish as much on their vacation as they planned to. And would you believe there's a sizable number of people who feel excited? They're anxious to get back to work.

That's such a simple example and the three most frequent responses are miles apart from each other. If you feel sad and don't say it and the other person feels excited about the same event, the other person will believe that since he or she feels excited, you feel excited too. And they'll act on it. They might even ask you to go out and celebrate. Can't you just see the potential for disaster? Just because you didn't express your feelings.

Here's another one "How do you feel when you get complimented in public?" Many people feel embarrassed. They wish they could vanish. Other people feel proud. They love basking in the limelight. So, if you're complimented in public and you feel embarrassed but don't say anything but your friend would feel proud if complimented in public, your friend might "assume" you feel proud as well and might heap positive remark upon positive remark on you causing you to shrink further into your shell, hating your friend more and more for "doing this to you."

Maybe your friend should have checked with you, (we'll cover that subsequently) but the responsibility certainly is yours. When you're having a feeling, share it!

And the last one, "How do you feel when you see a friend miss out on an opportunity?" Many people feel sad. They wanted better for their friend. Some people feel glad. Yes, it's their friend, but they believe that the friend had not put in all the effort that was necessary to insure a success, so they feel glad and also hopeful that the friend will learn from the experience. And a few people feel angry. They're not sure who they're angry at, or why they're angry, but they know they feel angry. How do you feel about it? However you feel, recognize that there are others who will feel similarly and still others who will feel differently.

Want to get to know your friends, family, colleagues and patients better? Ask them how they would feel in the following situations and see for yourself the wide range of responses you get.

- How do you feel when you walk into a room full of strangers?
- How do you feel when you're thanked for something by a colleague?
- How do you feel when your schedule has been changed and nobody even asked you?
- How do you feel when you thank someone and they say, "It's nothing?"

- How do you feel when your son or daughter hits a home run at a ball game?
- How do you feel when you try something and it doesn't work out?
- How do you feel when you go to a meeting with some friends and they leave with others, but without you?

If you asked others, you probably discovered that different people feel differently about the same kind of event. Now I hope you agree that, for a multitude of reasons, it pays to tell others what you're thinking and how you're feeling.

So, if in the past you might have seen someone knock over a soda bottle and would have said, "Look what you did ... you knocked over the soda" leaving it at that. Now you'll think about the "I" and the "you" and change your comment to, "Look what happened, the soda has been knocked over." And finally, because you've learned to express feelings you'll put it all together and say, "Look what happened, the soda has been knocked over. I feel so frustrated because I just cleaned that area a few minutes ago."

See it all now? The focus is important to defuse, but it's also important to express your feelings — and it can be done.

Another example would be instead of saying, "Wow, what a meeting." Now you can say, "Wow, you sure ran a wonderful meeting. I feel exhilarated." Catch the difference? The first part of the example focuses on the meeting and doesn't really express a reaction to it. The enlightened approach focuses on the other person because the meeting was so positive and adds the speaker's personal feeling. The other person feels great, they know your opinion (great meeting) and your feelings round out the flavor of the communication exchange.

Here are a few other examples. How would you change the following to include both a diffused focus and your feelings?

"Haven't you taken your lunch break yet?"

"You should have called me and reminded me that I was late for our appointment."

"There are some soccer games today and my son and daughter will be playing, so you'll have to finish up."

"Darn elevator, doesn't it ever come when it's needed?"

Levels of Communication

Superficial impersonal thoughts

Significant impersonal thoughts

Superficial personal thoughts

Significant personal thoughts

Feelings

A feeling is neither right nor wrong, IT JUST IS!!

We must tell them how we feel or *they will guess anyway*

To ignore feelings is like ignoring a warning light that indicates that an electric circuit is

OVERLOADED

CHAPTER SEVEN

Reflection of Feelings

"You seem angry..."

"Your frame of reference is the aggregate of all you have experienced, all you have learned, all you have seen and all that you have been told. There are people with similar frames of reference, and this makes it easier for them to communicate with you, but no two people have identical frames of reference."

Elaine Estervig Beaubien, Edgewood College, Madison, WI, writing in Tidbits, Tips & Tales

It's one thing to reveal your feelings. You're in control. You can choose to do it or not to do it. You know the benefits and consequences of each. What about other people? They might not have read this book. They might not have attended any workshop. They're having feelings too. Some people will be able to express those feelings and others won't. Yet, you need to know their feelings if you are to understand the full depth of their communication. What are your options when you suspect there's a feeling behind what someone is telling you but they're not saying it?

Guess

You can guess, like so many others do, but you know the problem with this one. You guess their feeling based on your reactions, on your past experiences and on your values, which may or may not match theirs. So you may guess wrong!

Ask them

You can ask them, "How does that make you feel?" This will work quite well with someone who understands feelings, who usually expresses them, but just didn't express them this time. They'll tell you their feelings. But those who usually don't share their feelings will generally feel "uncomfortable" when you ask and launch into a long description of facts. Or they might start their sentence with "Well, I feel that ..." and then give you their thoughts.

Tell them

"Don't tell them what they're feeling. It doesn't work."

You can tell them what feeling you think they're having and ask them to justify by saying something like, "Why are you so angry?" Please notice, you have made an "assumption" that they are angry, and now you are asking them to either justify or explain. This generally leads to trouble. They feel defensive and under the gun, like they've been caught and have to wriggle free. Often times they'll fight, by saying, "Who said I'm angry? What gives you the right to decide how I am feeling? You're not that smart yourself you know." Generally, this leads to another defense by you like, "Well you sure look angry. I can read people you know." And so on, and so on, and so on. Just a suggestion, don't tell them what feeling they're feeling. It doesn't work.

Reflect them

The ideal option is to reflect them and then check your perception. The skill of reflection requires that we act like a mirror, reflecting back to the speaker our perception of their feelings. Notice, we're not sure what they're feeling, we're not that smart, we can't get into their head or heart and we aren't sure we react to events the same way they do. But we are entitled to our belief, which forms the basis of the reflection.

We do it tentatively because we're really not sure, and then we check to see if our perception is accurate. It sounds like, "You seem angry. Are you?" Notice, we don't tell them they are angry, because we're not sure. We don't ask them why they're angry, because we're not sure. But we believe they are angry so tentatively we say, "You seem angry." Notice how tentative "seem" is. We could also say "appear" or "sound" or "look." Note that all three are tentative. Then we check our perception with, "Are you?" Then it's back to them. They don't have to defend themselves. They don't have to explain. They have a wide open option of saying "yes," "no," "kind of" or anything else they choose.

If they say yes, they will often tell you more about it, and not only will you learn details and get the full flavor of the event, but you will have been of tremendous service to the other person. You helped them express or verbalize a feeling and you know how beneficial that is. If they just say yes but don't say anything further, be a listener and offer yourself by saying, "Tell me about it. I'll listen."

If they say "no," honor their statement. This is not the time to argue, to offer evidence or force a confrontation. Mirrors don't fight, they just reflect. If the other person doesn't agree with the mirror, that's okay. Let them be. However, if they ask you why you think they're angry, stick to the facts. (We'll review "fact description" as a skill in a subsequent chapter).

When do we have an opportunity to "reflect feelings?" All day. For the patient who is talking louder than they normally do. Rather than say, "You don't have to shout," which is bound to embarrass them or start an argument, reflect them and say, "You seem annoyed. Are you?" They might say yes and tell you more about their feeling, or they might deny it, because in reality, their talking louder is the event and you interpreted it as annoyance, but not everyone does. For the patient who is telling you about their next appointment and you see a small smile on their face, be a mirror, reflect and say, "You look content. Are you?"

> "They needed to be able to express that feeling and you gave them that opportunity."

You've done them a great service. They'll probably tell you how relieved they are that their illness is not what it was first thought to be, and that they'll be coming back for a follow up and not to arrange surgery, etc. They needed to be able to express that feeling and you gave them that opportunity when you reflected. That patient will feel so good, so relieved and so thankful. They may tell you, they may not. They may tell others and they may not, but they'll certainly think that they've been treated wonderfully at your group.

If you think that a patient is feeling disappointed, use the reflection skill, the and say, "You sound disappointed. Are you?"

Keep noticing the tentativeness of each reflection and how the perception check puts it so gently and easily into their domain. They don't feel threatened, instead they feel secure.

And when people tell you their feelings, listen. In fact, the only thing there is to do is listen. There is no need to agree or disagree. Remember, it's their feeling and they're entitled to it. There will be time later to talk about facts that lie underneath the feelings, but for now, listen.

When they seem to be done, don't rush in with advice. There is no advice for a feeling. Don't rush in with a negation either. Many a nurse has told a patient, "Don't be afraid, Dr. Jones is an excellent doctor."

Whether the doctor is excellent or not, that's not the point. The point is that the patient is frightened and you can't tell them not to be. Want to prove it to yourself?

Forget about doctors and surgery for a moment. You're too close to it and too professional. Think of something that does frighten you. Is it the dark? Is it heights? Is it congested highway driving? Whatever it is, just imagine yourself in that precarious situation right now. Imagine you've told me about this feeling and I say to you, "Don't be afraid. There's a railing at the top of the building. Just hold on. You can't fall off. Don't be afraid."

Could you turn your feeling off? Of course not, and neither can the patient.

Here's another example that is sure to work with over 80 percent of the readers. Imagine a classroom. Imagine me walking to the chalkboard, taking my piece of chalk at the straight end, not the pointed end and placing that flat end against the chalkboard. Don't be afraid, don't be squeamish, it will only last for a couple of seconds. I take the chalk and draw it across the blackboard slowly, producing a ...

How are you reacting right now? Do you have goose bumps running up and down your body? Could you suppress it just because I told you to and that I'd only be dragging that square-ended chalk across the blackboard for a couple of seconds? I doubt it. Could you suppress it just because I told you to and that thousands of people don't mind it (I don't mind it) and that you shouldn't either? I doubt it.

So when someone tells you a feeling, listen — just listen. When they're through telling you, thank them for telling you because they have just shared with you at the highest level of communication, the feeling level, and they probably will think of you in a different way from now on.

The only appropriate response to someone who shares a feeling is, "Thank you." You could also add, "Tell me more."

Quite often there is quite a bit more but people are hesitant to share unless they feel safe and know you'll accept them. When you say thank you, they feel safe. When you ask them to tell you more, they feel accepted.

How lucky you both are. The other person is lucky because they get a chance to share their feelings with someone who accepts them and their feelings for what they are — feelings — with no judgments, just acceptance. How lucky they are to have you. How lucky you are to have had a chance to use this skill and establish a relationship with a patient who will probably come back for a lifetime because they are getting from your facility what they get from no other one — that personal touch on a feeling level.

Finally, they may ask you for your comment. They may ask, "Have you ever experienced something like this?" or "How do you react to ...?" Remember, this is not the time to lecture. Instead, this is an ideal time to associate. Don't tell them no. Even though it's in direct response to their question, it tends to separate. Tell them "Yes," in a qualified way.

I am not suggesting you lie. I am suggesting you associate. Here's how. When they ask you if you would have been angry at whatever they described and you really would have been say, "Yes, absolutely. I've felt anger just like that too." When they ask you if you would have been angry at whatever they described and you really wouldn't have been, say, "I know what anger is. I have lived with the same feeling as you did (that's your association. They know you understand them and have been where they've been), but my anger was caused by other circumstances than the one you described."

If you can associate with both the event and the feeling, great, tell them so, but if you've felt that feeling but never because of what caused it for them, associate with the feeling only. Don't tell them why you don't react the way they do. They didn't ask you for that information. Remember the four needs of people in communication — their need to hear your point of view comes third. They wanted your point of view, but not on everything, just on the topic they presented.

A nurse told me about a woman who was shaking in her prep room. The nurse said to her, "You look afraid. Are you?" The woman looked up, burst into tears, and went on to tell the nurse she was afraid of dying because she hadn't made peace with her family. As she spoke her voice climbed in crescendo, in uncontrolled sobs. When the nurse took her blood pressure it had shot sky high. The surgery was canceled and doctor told the nurse how thankful he was. If that patient had never had a chance to express her feelings, there was no telling how her body would have reacted under anesthesia while in surgery.

Picture the events that take place at your facility. A colleague telling you that they couldn't get the day off that they wanted to. "You seem frustrated. Are you?" might be an appropriate reflection.

Picture the colleague telling you about the positive outcome of an inspection of her division. "You sound proud. Right?" might be an appropriate reflection.

Notice, we substituted "right" for "are you." Now that you understand the concept of tentativeness and perception check, you don't have to be bound to the words given earlier. Whatever you recognize as a tentative statement qualifies for the first part of the reflection. Whatever you recognize as simple questioning qualifies for the perception check.

Here's another example:

Picture the patient who is telling you about not being able to find the laboratory. "Frustrating, huh?" may not be a complete sentence, but it surely qualifies as a reflection and perception check. Don't rush to just give the patient directions to the lab. Listen to them first and not just to the facts. Help them with their feelings. When you listen they feel good. Then, associate with them. It's easy for me to say, "I know frustration. I've felt it before, just like you, when I couldn't find what I needed to find." Wow, they will be feeling like they've found a friend — you. And they'll probably sing the praises of your facility to everyone. Then, and only then would I offer directions to the lab.

Watch them as they leave. They'll have said thank you a hundred times not because of the directions, but because of the total treatment they received. They'll head off to the lab, a jaunt in their walk, a smile on their face and a perk to their spirits, just because you listened to them, reflected them, associated with them and finally helped them.

Sometimes they'll negate your reflection. That's not a negation of you, but a negation of your reflection. If you reflect and say, "You seem distracted. Are you?" they might respond, "No, not distracted, just pensive." And your response will always be, "Thank you for telling me. Do you want to tell me more? I'll listen."

If communication is a two-way exchange of thoughts, facts and feelings, and you can help the other person with their feelings, you will have enhanced the total process. They may not recognize what you've done, but they will feel better for it and recognize you for your participation in the process, a process which they may not enjoy with too many other people, maybe not even with anyone else.

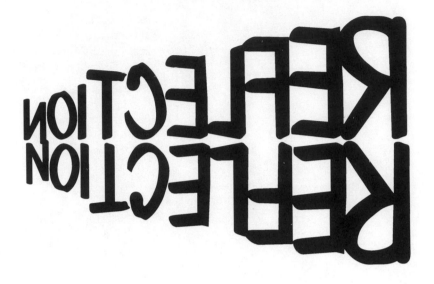

You seem _____ .

Are you?

CHAPTER EIGHT

Fact Description

"Just the facts, ma'am."

"No generalization is wholly true,
not even this one."

Oliver Wendell Holmes Jr.,

U.S. Surpreme Court Justice

"The facts ma'am, just the facts." That's what Jack Webb kept saying week after week, as he portrayed Sergeant Joe Friday on Dragnet as he searched for information to solve cases. Not that opinions weren't important, but he made it clear there was a time and place for each. In fact, there were times he specifically asked for opinions. After a person had told him a fact, Friday would ask, "And why do you think that happened?"

So it is in the total communication process. There are times we want facts, just facts, and we will reach our own conclusions. Other times we want facts and opinions and there are also times when there aren't any hard facts to go with so we entertain as many opinions as we can get.

What is important is that we recognize the place for each and the way to differentiate one from the other. Facts are measurable. We can see them, touch them and weigh them. The clock said 4 p.m., that's a fact. Even if the clock is inaccurate, the fact is, it said 4 p.m. Note the difference between "The clock said 4 p.m." and the statement "It was 4 p.m."

Seem minor? Then imagine you're working with an employee and you're trying to determine when they performed a certain test. If another employee tells you "they did it at 4 p.m.," and that represents a 45 minute delay which is unsatisfactory, you, the administrator might be very upset with the delay ... when in reality there might have been no delay whatsoever.

The person who told you it was 4 p.m. was giving you their opinion because the only fact available was that the clock said it was 4 p.m. What if we now discover that the clock is not accurate. In fact, the clock is 45 minutes fast. That would mean the test was done at 3:15 which would represent a timely performance. How can we determine this?

Joe Friday might have approached by saying, "When was the laboratory test done?"

"Don't jump to conclusions. And if others jump to conclusions don't allow their conclusions to interfere with your search for facts."

"It was done at 4 p.m."

"What makes you so sure?"

"The clock said it was 4 p.m."

"In other words, until we know if that clock was accurate, we only know that it said 4 p.m. Do you know about the accuracy of the clock?"

"Not really. I just assumed it was accurate."

"Let's check it against others."

Don't jump to conclusions. And if others jump to conclusions, don't allow their conclusions to interfere with your search for facts. Watch out for motives too. That is, don't be influenced by people's opinions about motives until you check out the facts and then evaluate the facts and opinions. For example:

Frank says to you, "Jim purposely dropped that beaker." Don't get sucked in to where you begin your conversation with Jim by asking, "Jim, why would you do such a destructive thing?" First, let's determine if he really dropped it. We need to determine the facts. We know the beaker is broken. We know it's lying on the ground, but did Frank see Jim drop it, or did he hear the crash and come in and see Jim standing over it.

Paraphrasing helps here. So, in our search to get the facts, when Frank tells you, "Jim purposely dropped that beaker," you could paraphrase and say, "In other words you were standing right there and saw it happen."

Frank might say, "Yes," in which case we still need more information, or he might say "No, but I heard a crash, came running in and saw him standing right over it." If he says "no" then we need to check out the possibility that Jim may not even have been holding the beaker at all. He may have been walking by the bench and knocked it over or he may not have been anywhere near the beaker when it fell, for whatever cause, and he came running over to see what happened. Searching for facts, dealing with facts is essential in any employee-related confrontations.

Let us now imagine that Frank says, "Yes, I was standing right there and saw it happen." Now we have facts as perceived by Frank. We still don't know that Jim purposely dropped it. It might have been an accident. It might have been that Jim had two things in his hands and lost control. Even if we accept as a fact that Jim dropped it because he admits it, we still cannot accept as fact that he dropped it on purpose. That needs further checking.

Another example:

The patient's chart reads, "Mr. Green is allergic to penicillin and is afraid of injections." Seems like two facts, doesn't it?

    1. allergic to penicillin; and

    2. afraid of injections.

But before you see the patient you decide to check with Nurse Smith about the notations, just to check the facts.

You: "Nurse Smith, I see you noted on Mr. Green's chart 'allergic to penicillin.' How do you know that?"

Nurse Smith: "He told me so himself."

You: "Thank you. I also see you noted that he is afraid of injections. How do you know that?"

Nurse Smith: "That's obvious. He was scheduled for flu and pneumonia shots. He canceled one appointment, then a second and even a third. Obviously he was canceling because he's afraid of injections."

You: "Thank you." (Suggestion: double check that with him directly.)

You: "Mr. Green, I notice you were scheduled for an appointment on the 8th, which was canceled, an appointment for the 10th which was canceled and an appointment on the 14th, which was also canceled. Are we scheduling these appointments at inappropriate times for you?

Did you notice the application of "I" and "You?"

Mr. Green: "No, not at all. You see, I was sick. I wish I had taken the flu shot earlier, but didn't, so would you believe it I got knocked for a loop by the flu. That's why I couldn't keep those appointments. In fact, give me my pneumonia shot now. I sure want to prevent that."

You: "Thank you for telling me that. Any fear of the injection?"

Mr. Green: "Of course not! Are you kidding?"

So much for a conclusion based on cancellations. The rule should be: Check it out before you enter it as fact. Even if it appears in the chart, check out facts vs. opinion.

Sometimes, even if you check for facts and are satisfied with the response, it's possible there are facts lying under the apparent facts that throw a different light on things. That's why it's necessary not only to check for facts, but also to always be prepared to use all your other communications skills. For example:

You: "Jim, I need someone to come in early this weekend to get things set up for the Open House. Know anybody for the job?"

Jim: "Sure, Charlie. He loves to come in early." (Better check your facts.)

You: "Thanks. What makes you say that?"

Jim: "Charlie told me so himself. He said he loves to come in early."

Can't beat that — actual first person evidence of facts.

You: "Thanks again Jim. I'll ask Charlie right now."

(The scene shifts)

You: "Charlie, I need someone to come in early this weekend to get things set up for the Open House. I heard you love to come in early, so I'm asking you. Okay?"

If Charlie says okay, it's a done deal. If he says he can't make it, well, the facts were accurate, the timing was wrong. But there's still another possibility which we will consider in the next chapter.

But for now, we realize that facts are essential in dealing with patients, with colleagues and with staff. It's our job to make sure we separate fact from opinion and verify the facts before we make our final acceptance.

CHAPTER NINE

Words and Music

"I've never been happier—WHY?!"

"During World War II, the Civil Defense authorities had posters printed which read: "Illumination must be extinguished when premises are vacated." When President Franklin D. Roosevelt saw these signs he exclaimed, "Why can't they say 'Put out the lights when you leave'?""

The road to the total communication bliss is paved with stories of success and stories of obstacles. In this chapter we'll deal with a potential obstacle. But first, let's ask:

- Does anybody listen? You do!
- Does anybody care? You do!

You show you're listening by applying the skills of active listening. You show you care, that you understand, by applying the skill of paraphrasing.

You understand the difference between their expression of facts, their expression of ideas and their expression of feelings. Not only do you recognize all this when they are talking but you've even learned how to "communicate" when you've got the floor. Most of the time, people say what they mean. But if and when there's informational confusion, the paraphrase always comes to the rescue.

But what if the "confusion" isn't informational. What if it's visceral, that is, you just get the feeling that what they're saying (their words) isn't matched by the way they're saying it (their music). When their words are matched by their music, that's symphonic. All players are playing the same melody, on the same key, they started at the same time and they are on beat. It's a pleasure to listen to — it's consistent, it's believable. All communication modules are in sync.

But when their words are not matched by their music, that's cacophony. All players are not playing the same melody, they're not in the same key, they did not start at the same time, nor are they in beat. It's hard on the ears and we strive to get away. All of the communication modules are not in sync.

So when someone tells you about a success story, listen to their words and their music too. Their voice might reflect a "lift." Their face might show a smile. Their hands might be open. Their body, their voice and their words would be playing together, in concert — a symphony — and you can believe it all. However, there might be a time when the words say one thing and other parts of the body seem to be saying something else. They

"There might be a time when the words say one thing and other parts of the body seem to be saying something else."

might be verbally saying how happy they are with something but their voice is trailing off, their face looks sad and their shoulders slump.

Rule: When the words and the music don't match ...

1. Don't believe the words;
2. Don't believe the music; instead
3. Check it out and be tentative when you do.

For example: Suppose you had just asked Jim, one of your employees, if he could come in early tomorrow. He looked up for a moment, then grimaced and said in a resigned tone, "Yes, I suppose so."

The words said yes but, to your ears, the music said something less than yes. What do you do?

Check it out. How?

By describing the facts, the conclusions you've drawn and then checking your perceptions and conclusions. It might sound like, "Jim, I heard you say 'yes,' but I also saw what I thought was a grimace and heard what I thought was resignation in your voice, like your voice and your body seem to be saying less than yes. Am I right?" Notice the fact description. "Jim, I heard you say yes, but I also saw what I thought was a grimace and heard what I thought was resignation in your voice." Notice the tentativeness of the perception and conclusion. Not only the use of the word "seem," but there also isn't an accusation that the voice and body were saying "no," just "less than yes." Remind you of "reflections?" And finally, the perception check, "Am I right?"

And if Jim says, "yes," what do we respond?

Think about it for a minute. Right! "Thank you for leveling with me. Tell me about it. I'll listen."

It may turn out that Jim had to take a child to school the next morning but has difficulty turning you down. After all, you are his boss and many employees find it difficult to say no to their boss.

Remember fact description? Remember we found out that Charlie loved to come in early because he said those very words to Jim. Let's continue with our scenario:

You: "Charlie, I need someone to come in early this weekend to get things set up for the Open House. I've heard you love to come in early, so I'm asking you. Okay?"

Charlie: "Me? This weekend? Oh ... Uh ... Well ... Uh ...Oh, (resignedly) I suppose so."

If you accept that, it appears you'll have your person for the weekend. But it sure sounds like the words and music don't match. Let's apply this newly learned skill to this scenario and say:

You: "Charlie, I heard you say, "I suppose so," but it sure sounded like you didn't care to. Please tell me about it."

Charlie: "Well, you see, I come in early every day. I love to because I have to take my kids to school and they start real early so instead of having to waste time before normal working hours, I come in early. I'm ready, I'm available and it means I don't waste any time. But you see, Saturday and Sunday are the only days I get to sleep late. I'll come in if it's absolutely necessary, but I'd much rather sleep in, get caught up, so I can get up early the rest of the week."

You: "Thank you, Charlie. I appreciate your honesty. Let me try someone else."

Charlie: "And if you can't find anyone else, let me know. I'll be available if absolutely necessary. In fact, maybe we could split. Someone takes Saturday early and I'll take Sunday, or vice versa."

You: "Thanks Charlie. I appreciate your offer. I'll get back to you if I need you ... and thanks again."

So you see, the facts given to you by Jim were right. Charlie did tell Jim that "he loves to come in early." Jim had been reporting the facts, as he knew them but (let's do a mini-review here), if Jim had paraphrased Charlie in the beginning, Jim might have said, "You mean every day, even if it were a weekend?" And no doubt Charlie would have responded, "Weekends? No, on weekends I love to sleep in. Only on weekdays. In fact, only on days when my kids are in school do I like to come in early."

The wonders and beauty of communication are that it's virtually never too late to get clarity. Yes, Charlie could have said it fully himself at the very beginning by saying, "I love to come in early, but only on days when my kids are in school." But he didn't. No problem, Jim could have paraphrased him, as outlined earlier.

But he didn't. No problem, because when you finally did ask Charlie the question, you were alert enough to pick up that his words and music didn't match. Use this skill to check it out and get to the real bottom of things. It's never too late to get things straight! There's always an appropriate skill that will get it done!

Does anybody listen? Does anybody care? Yes, you do!

But don't just assume that because the words and music don't match that the music is correct. Quite often the music is correct, but if you don't check it out, you run the risk of recreating this next experience in your own facility.

Nurse: "Jane, we can get you an appointment with Dr. Smith on next Wednesday, the 10th at 3 p.m. Is that OK?"

Jane: (Pensive ... eyes arched ... appears to be going through a painful decision-making process) says "OK, Wednesday the 10th at 3 p.m."

Nurse: (Having observed what took place and heard the okay, believes the words and music are not matching. She doesn't check it out. She believes the music) and says, "Oh, let me look for something else. I have one here approximately a week later on Thursday the 18th at 9 a.m. Is that better?"

Jane: (Angry) "Why are you driving me crazy? You asked me a question about an appointment on the 10th. I said yes, and then you go and change it to the 18th. Can't you believe what I told you the first time?"

Suppose you were in this dilemma. What would you do now?

Maybe you'd be asking yourself, "How did I get into this? Why did I ever listen to her words and music. I should have just taken her "okay," scheduled the date and if she couldn't make it, that's her tough luck." Maybe you'd even talk to her and explain why you did why you did. But I hope you wouldn't be doing either of those.

Whatever the cause, whatever just took place, it's not important. We must put that all aside for the moment. It sounds like Jane is angry, but she is not expressing a feeling. She's jabbing a question at you. So before you respond to her question, before you defend yourself, just think back to the chapter on reflections.

This situation now fits that bill perfectly, so I hope you drop all discussion of the appointment for the moment and reflect, "Jane, you seem angry. Are you?"

There's no point explaining, there's no point conversing there's no point in trying to be logical right now. Jane may be having a feeling — anger — and until she has a chance to express it, there's no way for logic, the appointment or for the conversation to move on.

So there you see that the skill of reflections can be called for, any time, under any circumstance, and when it is needed, it takes priority.

But ideally, this scene won't happen because you wouldn't have allowed it to happen. Let's go back to the very beginning. Instead of believing the music and acting on it, the nurse will utilize the skill of words and music.

Nurse: "Jane, we can get you an appointment with Dr. Smith on next Wednesday, the 10th at 3 p.m. Is that okay?"

Jane: (Pensive, eyes arched, appears to be going through a painful decision-making process says), "Okay, Wednesday the 10th at 3 p.m."

Nurse: (Having observed what took place and heard the okay, believes the words and music are not matching. So she checks it out by saying, "Jane, I heard you say okay, but you looked like you were in pain with it all, like it might be impossible to do. Is that it?" See the fact description? See the sharing of conclusions? See the tentativeness? See the perception check?

Now the nurse might have heard: "Oh thank you for picking up on that, but it's okay, really. You see I had promised someone to meet them for lunch on the 10th, and I was figuring how we could have lunch, finish and still allow me to get to this office by 3 p.m. But, the appointment is far more important to me so I'll either schedule the lunch half an hour earlier or move it to another day. But I definitely want that doctor's appointment on the 10th at 3 p.m."

Can't you just hear the definitiveness of this statement? Can't you just hear the positive ring to the voice and see the hand point forward to punctuate? Now the words and music match. Believe it. She'll be there.

Often times when we perceive words and music not matching, it's because the speaker is trying to balance their activities. On the one hand your activity, on the other hand, something else they might have planned. It's not easy, but they're deciding. Sometimes, they'll say okay, but it will sound pained, and your reflection will help them tell you that no, it's not okay. That even though they said okay, they would much prefer to move it to another time ... so your use of the skill helped prevent a possible no show or cancellation on the 10th.

On the other hand, there will be times when they'll say okay, it will sound pained and your words/music reflection will help them tell you that it really is okay, they just needed to work something out in their own head. The pain was uncertainty and now it's turned into certainty.

Two good things just happened:

1. The appointment will be filled, not no-showed or canceled; and
2. The patient will be thankful for a nurse like you, for helping them reconcile their own indecision.

Sadly, many professionals don't hear the music. They hear only the words and act on it, regardless of the music. That works well when they are in harmony but it fails miserably when they are in discord.

Sadly, other professionals do listen and do hear words and music. But when the words and music don't match, they don't know which to believe. There have been times they've believed the words, but been burned. There have been other times when they've believed the music, and been burned so they guess.

Congratulations! Now you won't have to guess. You know all the requisite components of this skill and now you'll be prepared for either of these following, often seen examples:

- You notice a colleague studying a report. Your colleague seems perplexed, so as a friend you ask, "Is everything okay?" Your colleague looks up with a kind of blank look and comments, "What? Oh, yes, uh, yes." What would you say or do now?
- A patient asks if you could help them cap a urine specimen. You say, "Sure" (words and music matching please), cap the bottle and then ask, "Is there anything else?" They smile, what appears uncomfortably to you and answer, "No, I guess that's it." What would you say or do now?

Common occurrences, right? In both cases, don't believe the words, don't believe the music — check it out.

1. Describe the facts as you saw them. "You used the word, 'xx', but, I saw your face do this (show a grimace)";
2. Share your conclusion. "It looks to me that it isn't all clear or all settled";
3. Be tentative. Use your tentative vocabulary; and
4. Check your perception.

The professional who knows and applies the skill of words and music has fewer plans changed by others at the last minute, enjoys better rapport and earns the reputation of being able to "get to the bottom of things." It's easy to get to the bottom when you are able to separate conflicting components and then let the other person lead you there.

When words and music match
SYMPHONY

When words and music don't match
CACOPHONY

CHECK IT OUT

CHAPTER TEN

Asking Questions

"The first function of the executive is to
develop and maintain a system
of communication."

Chester I. Bernard, President, USO,
Functions of the Executive, Harvard, 1938

Why is it that some people ask questions and get answers, while others ask questions and get defenses? Why is it that some people can ask questions and people stay calm, while others ask questions and everyone gets edgy? Why is it that some people ask questions and reach an end point, while others ask questions and go on and on?

Could it be that skilled communicators signal their motive before asking the question, while others do not? Could it be that skilled communicators ask questions that are easy to understand, while others do not? Could it be that skilled communicators use words that make the question easy to respond to, while others do not? Could it be that skilled communicators ask questions in a pattern, while others attack in staccato?

It could be one, two, three or all of these. Most people are wary when others ask them a question. They don't know what's coming so they feel defensive. They feel like they're under the gun (that's a simile). What can you do as a communicator to prevent placing the other person in that position? Many things.

Don't ask unless you really want to know

Don't ask a question unless you really want to know the answer unless you really intend to use the information. Remember, ever since we were children, we've been asked questions that merely serve as the beginning of a series of escalating questions, so every time we hear them today, we squirm. For example:

We came home late for dinner and mom asked us, "Where were you?" Did she ever really want to know the answer? Rarely. That was just the first question of a series of escalating questions that eventually got us sent to our room without dinner.

Now, we come late to work, and the supervisor asks us, "Why are you late for work?" Is there any answer that will satisfy the supervisor? Do they really want to know? Generally, not. They're just using the question to get to their tirade about the importance of being on time, etc.

So people condition themselves to be wary any time a question comes their way. They condition themselves to believe that the other person really doesn't want to know the answer. Sometimes, it appears the other person does want to know the answer, but they don't tell why, which leads to the fear of questions with hidden motives.

Tell them why you're asking

Give them your motive. Tell them why you're asking. It doesn't make it totally safe for the other person, but it alleviates some of their fear.

Remember, ever since we were children, we've been asked questions with hidden motives, and we squirmed every time we heard them. For example: When playing with siblings, a brother or sister might ask, "Do you have any postage stamps from Australia?" Immediately the question runs through our mind, "Why are they asking?" Do they want to trade stamps with you? Do they want you to give them some stamps? Do they want to give you some stamps? Why are they asking? What's their motive?

A gentleman once told me that he had a boss who would ask him, "Mike, what are you doing Saturday afternoon?" Oh, what a dilemma this was for him. You see, he knew his boss had season tickets for the Atlanta Braves baseball team and they were right in the middle of a pennant race. Was the boss asking because he wanted to take Mike to the game? Or, was the boss asking because he wanted Mike to come in and work that Saturday? As Mike told it to me, "If the boss wanted me to go to the game with him Saturday, I was free — and even if I had something planned, I'd cancel it for the box seats he had. But, if the boss wanted me to work on Saturday, I was busy, very busy. Oh how I hated those questions. Why didn't he make it easier for me and just tell me why he was asking?"

Or what about this one. Someone comes to you and asks you how many of the older chairs you have in your office. Do you wonder why they're asking?

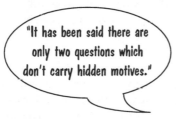

"It has been said there are only two questions which don't carry hidden motives."

We'll deal with how we would handle these later, but for now, can you see how uncomfortable it is to be confronted by a question with a hidden motive? People tell me it frustrates them, so don't do it to them. Tell them why you are asking.

It has been said there are only two questions which don't carry hidden motives that people accept without fear and they are:

1. What time is it?; and
2. Where's the bathroom?

(Even question #1 might have a hidden motive to it!)

Tell people why you're asking. It can be as simple as, "Janet, I'm putting together a log of the hobbies of members of our staff, so I need to ask you, 'What's your hobby'?"

Compare that approach with the one so often used, "Janet, what's your hobby?" When you tell the other person your motive for asking, they find it easier to respond. This is not to say it's totally easy, but it's easier than if no information is given at all.

When questioning a patient, don't just start asking, "When was the first time you noticed the pain?" Even though they are in a medical office, they need to hear you say, "Jim, I need certain information to help me diagnose so we can get you started on the road to recovery. Tell me, When was the first time you noticed the pain?"

There may be times when you cannot reveal the reason for asking. There were times when I was seeking corporate information but I was not at liberty to reveal why. Don't run away from it. If you can't reveal the motive, then at least reveal the fact that you know you're not revealing the motive. Once again, it doesn't totally relieve the pressure, but it does reduce it. It might sound like this:

"Lionel, I'm gathering some information and I wish I could tell you the reason for it, but I can't. However, I can tell you that this information is essential to my completing the project, so I need to know: What is the highest temperature you've ever noticed in the laboratory?"

Not as good as totally revealing the motive, but far better than just saying, "Lionel, what is the highest temperature you've ever noticed in the laboratory?" That question will undoubtedly cause a sudden rise in Lionel's temperature and blood pressure. He doesn't know why you're asking.

Ask the question in the positive

As we've already seen, questions are hard enough to cope with in and of themselves, without the question compounding the problem. Questions in the negative are hard to understand. The other person doesn't quite know how to answer and the answer quite often leads to a misunderstanding. For example:

"Robert, you're not in favor of the new vacation plan?"

That's a negative question. In theory, my grammarian friends tell me, that a "yes" means "no" and a "no" means "yes."

They explain that if I answer "yes," it means that I affirm that I am "not" in favor of the new vacation plan. In other words, I'm against it. Whereas, they continue, if I answer "no," it means that I am in favor of the new vacation plan, for I am saying "no" to the "not," the double negative being a positive, so when I answer "no," I'm saying I am in favor of the new vacation plan.

Confusing isn't it?

Now you understand the reality of the rule. Ask the question in the positive. The question now would be asked, " Robert, are you in favor of the new vacation plan?"

It isn't any better if you ask the patient, "You haven't finished the medication, have you?" Here even my grammarian friends disagree. Some say, the yes or no response applies to the major clause, "haven't, while others say it applies to the minor clause, "Have you?" It doesn't make any difference which of them is grammatically correct, if one of them was the questioner and the other the responder, there would never be a clear understanding if the medication had been taken or not.

So don't ask the question in the negative, even if it's got a positive clause to it. Simply ask, "Have you finished the medication?" Clearly, now a "yes" means "yes" and a "no" means "no."

Another example: You ask a colleague, "Aren't you done with the chart?" Grammatically this expands to "Are you not done with the chart?" Yes means I'm still working on it, I'm not done. No means I'm finished, I'm done.

Suppose you were waiting to work on the chart yourself. Are you a grammarian? Is the other person a grammarian? Does "yes" mean "yes," or does "yes" mean "no?" Don't bother trying to figure it out. Ask the question in the positive, "Are you done with the chart?" "Yes" means "yes" and "no" means "no."

What other examples of negative questions can you think of that you might have asked, or that might have been asked of you?

When you ask the question, you're in control. From now on make sure you don't ask a negative question, ask a positive one instead. As for what to do when someone asks you a negative question? We'll cover that next chapter.

Avoid assumptive questions

This is the kind of question that makes an assumption and proceeds from that. The classic is, "When did you stop beating your wife?"

Notice, the assumption is made that beating has taken place, that it has stopped and now the only information that's wanted is "when."

"How could you close the lab without shutting down the incubator?" Notice, the assumption is that this person is the one who closed the lab and that they didn't shut down the incubator. Better check those assumptions first before posing the question.

What about, "Why did you cancel the appointment and schedule a new one four weeks later? Didn't you know that appointment was critical and that time was of the essence?" Sure looks like assumptions, multiple questions and accusations all rolled into one. How comfortable would the scheduling nurse be if you posed those at her? Do we know that she canceled the appointment? Whether she knew the appointment was critical or not it sure doesn't sound like you want the answer to that one. Sounds like you'll use whatever answer is given to launch into your own tirade.

And this scenario:

You're trying to convince a patient about a treatment regime but the patient resists. Finally, in frustration you ask, "Why can't you be more reasonable?" Assumptions, assumptions, assumptions. Do you really want an answer to that question? Is it the patient who needs to be more reasonable or could it be that you need to check the reasonableness of your proposal.

And finally:

An employee has just said something to a fellow employee which led to loud and angry words between the two, disrupting the flow of patient care in the office. You now have one of those employees sitting in a chair in your office and you ask, "What's wrong with you? Don't you know any better?" Assumptions, assumptions, assumptions. Do you really want answers to those questions? Has the employee already been found guilty before having a chance to say a word?

No more than one question per question

Just as confusing as the negative question is, so is the multiple question within the single question. It sounds something like this:

"Did you take medicine #1 as prescribed until it was finished, then start medicine #2 and do the urine specimen after one day on medicine #2?"

What is this poor patient supposed to do, answer "yes, yes, no?" It's too complicated. Make it easy on the patient. Break it down into different questions.

How about:

How would you like to be asked, "Will you be able to check Mr. Jones' file before he comes in and if it isn't complete call him and reschedule his appointment with you for next Thursday?" or,

"When did the pain begin, has it always been as severe and did the physical exercise help any?" and,

"Will you be closing the office tonight at 8 p.m.?" If you are the one who is closing the office, but the closing is at 7 p.m., ideally you should answer, "I'll close the office, but at 7 p.m. But if you just said, "yes" and they stopped by at 7:45 and found it closed, they might be upset.

The solution is simple. One question per question.

Know which kind of question to ask

Basically there are two kinds of questions, the open question and the closed question. The closed question is one where control is retained by the questioner. Closed questions are those where the answer is short, sometimes only one word, "yes" or "no." Control immediately reverts to the questioner. For example:

Did you go to the meeting? Yes or no?

Have you finished the project? Yes or no?

Because control immediately reverts to the questioner, responders usually find closed questions very threatening. They recognize they are out of control.

Other examples of closed questions focus on the use of certain words to start the question. For example:

A question which begins with the word "when." "When is your appointment?" "When will the meeting start?" "When will we get our paychecks?"

All of these questions can be answered quickly. One or two words, and then control reverts to the questioner.

A question which begins with the word "where." "Where is the report?" "Where will the meeting take place?" "Where is your X-ray?"

Again, notice that all of these questions can be answered quickly, often with one or two words and control then reverts to the questioner.

A question which begins with the word "who." "Who reads the X-ray?" "Who will cover the laboratory when Jim is on jury duty?" "Who examined you on the 11th?"

Once again, please notice that all of these questions can be answered quickly, still with one or two words, and control again reverts to the questioner.

This is not to say that closed questions are bad. Closed questions are neither good nor bad, they just are. But in order for us to be communication practitioners, we need to know which kind of questions exist and how to recognize them. Closed questions save time. Their answers are usually very short. Closed questions keep control in the hands of the questioner. Great for the questioner — somewhat uncomfortable for the responder. Closed questions are best used when there is specific information that is needed and the responder probably has the information. This does not relieve the questioner of the responsibility of "stating the motive" first. It makes it a little easier for the responder.

On the other hand, open questions allow far more leeway to the responder. Open questions may take a responder one minute to answer, five minutes or even 10 minutes. It depends on the question, the amount of information they have and the amount of information they wish to share. Like the closed question, open questions also focus on the use of certain words or different words, to start the question.

Questions beginning with "Why"

"Why did you stop taking the medication?" That question might be answered in a few words, or the patient might go into all kind of detail. Control is with the responder. "Why did the meeting run hours?" Once again, the answer might be as simple as "I don't know," but it also could provide a blow by blow detail of the disagreement that took place. Control is with the responder. "Why is Jim not here today?" Same kind of time frame possibilities. Control is with the responder.

Questions beginning with "What"

"What took place at the meeting?" The answer might be short and sweet, or it might be full of detail. But notice, control is with the responder. "What do you plan to do next?" "What are our alternatives?"

Questions beginning with "How"

"How did that happen?" See how the answer might be short and sweet or full of detail? See how control is with the responder? "How did the family react?" "How did the laboratory handle the emergency?"

Open questions are neither good nor bad, they just are. Closed questions are neither good nor bad, they just are. But we need to recognize that closed questions keep control with the questioner. They:

- gain specific information;
- take small amounts of time; and
- make   the responder feel uncomfortable.

"Whenever you ask a question have enough time available to wait for the answer."

Open questions transfer control to the responder. They:

- bring responses of unknown length;
- bring responses of unknown depth and knowledge; and
- sometimes bring discomfort to the questioner especially if the responder wanders and goes into more detail than the questioner wanted to know.

This leads to the next rule of asking questions:

Have enough time to wait for the answer

Whenever you ask a question have enough time available to wait for the answer. This makes the assumption that you want to know the answer. If that's true, leave time for the other person to supply it. There are some people (including doctors, nurses, receptionists, technicians, etc.) who have been known to ask a question, wait a moment for the answer, then wheel around and leave. There is one woman who reported that she found a way to cope with her doctor when he did that. After her doctor came into the room, this woman placed herself between the doctor and the door. She literally barricaded the door and now the doctor had to give her the time she wanted. That was her solution. Too many others find another solution — they leave the practice. The more open questions you use, the more time you will need.

Be silent

After you've asked the question, be silent. Wait for the answer. This again assumes you want the answer, and have time. If you don't want the answer, don't ask. If you don't have time, don't ask. But when you do have time and you do want the answer, wait for it.

The best way to wait for it is patiently. Be silent. You have no way of knowing what's going on in the mind of the other person. They may be thinking of the very information you seek. They may have the information you seek but may be deciding if they want to tell you. They may have the information you seek and be deciding how best to phrase it, and to present it. We don't know what's going on in their minds so let's not interrupt them.

Some questioners are so impatient they give their responders a brief moment before they either move on, ask another question or rephrase the one that's on the table. Doctors have a notorious reputation for allowing their patients only a few seconds of "think time" before they move on. Teachers have a similar reputation and parents might be the worst offenders of all. Patients call that rude. They say, "If you asked me, wait until I answer."

I'm often asked, "How long should I wait?"

I can't offer a formula. I can tell you that I once asked someone a very complicated question. That person took five minutes to think. I almost died during the interim, but finally he turned in his chair, said, "Thank you for waiting," and gave me a complete well thought-out answer to the complex question.

"Yes, but some people just say nothing and hope the question will go away. What should I do then?" is another frequently asked question.

People who delay responding have learned that in most cases, it works. As children, they may have learned that when people asked them, "Where were you?" if they said nothing, they may not get dinner, they might be sent to their room — but they never told where they were, either. So they've learned that silence works for them.

Wait as long as you can and just before you think you will burst, just before you are about to say something else wait another 30 seconds. Almost invariably in that last 30 seconds, the other person starts speaking. And if that doesn't work, I interrupt the silence by saying, "I really do need to know the answer to that question John, so I'll wait," and then I even slap my hand over my mouth to let them know I won't speak any more, the ball is now in their court. Most of the time, the other person will answer.

No more than three questions per round

Recalling that people are nervous when asked questions, even if we ask the questions right, even if we tell our motives, then there has to be a maximum to which I wish to subject responders. I suggest that three be the maximum per round.

That means I can ask three questions before the responder gets a break. During that break I might paraphrase the responses, I might summarize, I might interject, but the pressure and the spotlight is taken off the other person.

"How long should the break be?" In boxing the break between rounds is one minute. That would be appropriate in communication, but 20 seconds is the least time I would accept as break time.

Represent both open and closed questions

Within any group of three questions that you ask, always have both kinds of questions represented. That simply means two opens and one closed or two closed and one open, but never three closed in a row or three opens in a row. Three closed in a row will surely have the responder squirming. Three opens in a row might have you squirming, but also will create the impression that you're on a witch hunt. So, mix the two and you'll get the information you need, you'll feel comfortable and so will the other person. It might sound like this:

You: "Jim, I didn't have a chance to get to the department meeting last Friday and I'm anxious to get the low down. Tell me, did you attend the department meeting last Friday?"

Jim: "Sure did."

You: "Great, then I'm talking to the right person. I'm anxious to know if I was the only one missing. Who else missed the meeting?"

Jim: "Just Charles and Harriet."

You: "Thanks. What took place at the meeting?"

Notice, a closed question (yes or no), a second closed question (who) followed by the open question (what).

As always, there is no guarantee that Jim will be comfortable under questioning, but did you notice how you first gave him your motive, then asked the first question? After the answer, a form of thanks, then the motive for the second question, followed by the question. After the answer, thank him (remember that one from five chapters back?) and then go on to the next question, giving the motive first.

"What if I've got someone on our staff that I avoid asking questions, not because they don't want to answer, not because they don't have the information, but because they are so darn long winded they take forever to answer."

Not usual, but not uncommon either. What do you do? Well, there are options:

1. Use more closed ended questions; and
2. Use your old friend, buying time.

Remember, when someone goes on and on, you do have the right to "buy time." Also remember the rule of "I" and "you."

1. Say their name. That will get them to stop. If they don't stop, just keep on repeating their name. They will finally stop;
2. Say something nice;
3. State the circumstances; and
4. Make an arrangement.

It might sound like this when someone keeps answering with more detail than you ever wanted.

1. "Jim ... Jim ... Jim." (He finally stops.);
2. "Jim, I certainly appreciate the effort you're putting forth to give me a complete answer;
3. "I guess I didn't ask the question correctly"; and
4. Let me rephrase it this way and see if I can do better."

Notice, you've managed to interrupt the answer, take responsibility for the problem, give them thanks for their effort, and make another attempt to get answers without all the details.

You can't blame them for trying. Look to yourself to changing the style and type of question with this kind of person. But, be careful, we don't want to discourage them because they're virtual fountains of information and always so willing to share it with us.

In summary, when asking questions follow these 10 steps:

1. Make sure you want to know the answer. Don't ask if you don't want to know;
2. Have enough time available to hear the answer;
3. State your motive;
4. Avoid assumptive questions;
5. Choose open and closed questions carefully. One question per statement. Ask the question in the positive;
6. Wait for the answer, give them time to answer;
7. Thank them for the answer;
8. If the question is closed, and many facts are involved, repeat them back for accuracy;
9. If the question is open, paraphrase the answer for understanding; and
10. Ask the next question but remember only three questions per round.

At the beginning of this chapter we asked:

Why is it that some people ask questions and get answers, while others ask questions and get defenses? Why is it that some people can ask questions and people are calm, while others ask questions and everyone gets edgy? Why is it that some people ask questions and reach an end point, while others ask questions and go on and on?

Could it be that skilled communicators signal their motive before asking the question, while others do not? Could it be that skilled communicators ask questions that are easy to understand, while others do not? Could it be that skilled communicators use words that make the question easy to respond to, while others do not? Could it be that skilled communicators ask questions in a pattern, while others attack in staccato?

It could be one, two, three or all of these. And now you know how to make sure you're one of the skilled communicators, getting answers not defenses, keeping people calm and using all the skill components of asking questions.

CHAPTER ELEVEN

Responding to Questions

"Not knowing the question, it was easy for him to give the answer."

Dag Hammerskjold

The shoe is on the other foot now. Instead of being the questioner, you're the responder. Someone is asking you a question. It would be ideal if they had already read Chapter 10 and every question they asked followed all of the rules of the chapter. But just in case the rules aren't followed, let's learn skills that will help. You do have options.

Answer the question

Obviously this is the easiest one of all. You're asked, you answer. Very simple with "yes" and "no" type questions. Generally they are easy to understand. Not necessarily so with other closed-type or open questions. Sometimes, they're not that easy to understand, so as part of option number one include the skill of paraphrasing. Whenever a question is asked, paraphrase it to make sure you understand it. There is no point in responding when the answer you'll be giving is not the information the questioner is looking for.

For example:

Question: "Who was at the meeting?"

This question seems simple and straightforward, but let us imagine there were 20 people at the meeting. Before you undertake the laborious task of naming every person, paraphrase by saying, "You mean who was there from our department?"

If they respond "yes," you've just saved yourself a lot of effort and saved the other person from a long list of names in which they weren't interested.

Question: "What are our alternatives?"

It is easy enough to start listing the alternatives, but maybe a little paraphrase could narrow it down, a paraphrase like, "You mean alternatives that could be implemented without any increase in staff?"

If they respond "yes," you've just saved yourself a lot of effort and saved the other person from a long list of alternatives that they might have regarded as impractical. Yes, I know they should have stated that at the very beginning of the question, but they didn't. That still doesn't prevent you from clarifying and being thankful that you used the skill.

Notice these examples are for questions that you're comfortable answering. What if there's a question with a hidden motive thrown at you? What now? Remember "What are you doing Saturday afternoon?" Remember "Do you have any postage stamps from Australia?" Remember "What's your hobby?" and "How many older chairs do you have in your office?"

It's a funny story with those chairs. This actually took place at a clinic. The person who was asked the question didn't know the motive, didn't know how to find out the motive, figured that the reason that information was needed was to see if she could spare an older chair, which she didn't want to give away. So in her response she purposely said three instead of four. Two weeks later a maintenance worker delivered three brand new chairs to her office and took the older ones away. She now complained that she had four older chairs, and wanted four new ones, but the maintenance worker's work order only showed three older chairs, so she only got three new ones. If only she had known. Of course she could have asked, "Why do you want to know?" and she might have gotten her answer. Or, she might have gotten what Mike got when dealing with his boss who asked him, "Mike, what are you doing Saturday afternoon?"

Mike: "Why do you ask boss?"

Boss: "Oh, just curious." Foiled? Not Mike, who quickly continued.

Mike: "You know boss, curiosity killed a cat" (hoping the boss would reveal the motive).

Boss: "I know, but I'm not a cat."

What other options beside answering did Mike have?

Paraphrase

Yes, we just learned about paraphrasing to get clarification. Here's a perfect chance to use it. Simply paraphrase and say, "You mean there's work to be done here at the office Saturday?" Maybe the boss will say, "Yes, and I was hoping you could cover it." Maybe not what you wanted to hear, but at least you know what the motive is and you can now answer as you see fit. Or maybe, just maybe, the boss might say, "No, I've got tickets to the ball game and was hoping you could come along."

See how easy the paraphrase works to uncover a motive? There is no need to panic, just paraphrase. It works just as well in the case of the "old chairs."

"You mean you need some chairs in another office?"

"No, we're replacing all old chairs with new ones."

"Oh, I've got four." (Carefully resist the temptation to say five.)

What about the Australian postage stamps? Paraphrasing works just as well to uncover the motive. It might sound like this:

"Do you have any extra postage stamps from Australia?"

"You mean so we can trade?"

Buy time

You remember this old friend. This skill works perfectly when you want to think about it, yet it doesn't offend the other person. The more complicated the question, the more appropriate the use. Remember, the other person has the advantage. They know what they want to know, they know why they want to know it and they asked the question at the moment they were ready to ask it. You, on the other hand, might have no idea why they are asking and your mind may not be right for thinking about it or responding, so you can respond:

"Mr. Robinson, thank you for asking. You certainly know how to take care of your health (that's the nice thing). But I don't have the information right at hand (status report). Let me check it out and get back to you in an hour. Okay?" (the next step).

There may be times an employee has been thinking about something for weeks on end and finally they come up with an idea, a suggestion for handling a given situation. They come to see you and tell you all about it, with great enthusiasm and then they ask, "Well, what do you think?" There you are ... stuck. But not really. Buying time works wonders here and literally builds on the fact that they've been thinking about it so long. The formula is the same and sounds like:

"Just because you ask me now does not mean I must answer now. I can buy time."

"Jane, my compliments to you. You certainly did a terrific job thinking this through from start to finish. It seems to me you must have spent weeks and weeks on this (they'll be nodding yes, both in appreciation of your compliment and in agreement with the time frame) and because you put in so much effort in preparing this suggestion, I need to give it the same kind of diligent thought you did (status). I won't take weeks and weeks, but let me think about it and I'll get back to you in 10 days, okay?" (the next step).

Here's a rule for self protection: Just because you ask me now does not mean I must answer now. I can buy time.

Alert: Beware of the telephone.

Whereas I seem to be able to control my timing when we're face to face, the telephone creates an entirely different scenario. It blurts its sound, and almost like a reflex, I answer. I pick it up, and there's someone on the other end who says, "Jacob, I must know ..." and they ask the question.

Normally, I am aware of the options I have, those listed earlier and those to come, and when we're face to face I have no difficulty in answering, or using the most appropriate option. But when the phone rings, it appears that almost all my preparation goes flying out the window.

The phone represents urgency, immediacy. The person asking the question adds to that scenario and I fall right into the trap. Oh how I wished I could have a tool that could drag back all the answers I gave that I wished I hadn't on the phone. I still don't have the tool, but I do have a little note hanging on my phone that says:

Just because someone asks me now doesn't mean I must answer now. I can buy time!

Use a repeating phrase

In our quest to find out someone's motive for asking a question a repeating phrase works wonders. It simply lets the other person know you've been listening and are anxious to respond, but, there's something missing. When you use the repeating phrase you simply repeat back to the questioner one or several words of the question, and let it hang there.

The questioner will invariably pick up the ball and elaborate, give their motive or divulge more. It sounds like:

Patient: "How did my EKG look compared to last time?"
You: "Compared to last time?"

The patient will invariably reveal that they are worried that it might have gotten worse, or that they are anxious to know if it has gotten better. But they will talk and then they'll pose the question again, but this time you'll understand their motive.

Another example:

Colleague: "How many patients did you handle yesterday?"

You: "Patients? Yesterday?"

The colleague will often advise that yesterday was such a busy day that he or she didn't have time to file the report that was necessary, etc. Then you will be in a much better position to answer.

Let us again state for the record, if you're comfortable, answer the question. Then there is no need to employ any option, just answer the question. You may or may not paraphrase for understanding, but, just answer the question.

However, if you're just not feeling comfortable with the question, if you're wondering why the question is being asked of you or you feel the pressure and want time to think about an answer, you now have options, and there are more.

Sounds like

Have you ever been asked a question and sensed there was "politicking" in the air, and you really didn't want to answer the question before finding out what the questioner thought on the subject? "Sounds like" works well here. After the question you simply acknowledge that your information on the topic is sketchy, but it sounds like the other person knows lots more so you ask them the very same question they asked you. It sounds like this:

Colleague: "What do you think about the new dress code slated to go into effect here next Thursday?"

You: "Sounds like you know so much more about it than I do. Please fill me in and then give me your thinking, okay?"

Chances are your colleague will give you all the details and then their opinion on the matter. Then you can answer, or buy time or say you'd prefer not to answer.

Another example:

Patient: "What's your opinion on the new noninvasive cardiology test to detect early atherosclerosis?"

You: "Sounds like you've done research on it. What have you found out and what do you think about it?"

The "sounds like" approach works and works well because you've complimented the person and acknowledged their expertise so they are more than willing to speak. They speak, and they even hold you in high esteem for giving them the opportunity. And it all started with them asking you a question.

Tell them "no comment"

"No comment" is a well-known type of reply in public circles. The person who has been questioned reserves the right not to answer the question. Assuming it's not a court of law, assuming the question is not being asked by your supervisor you may think it best to be quiet on the topic. Assuming you have that right, all that need be said is, "I appreciate your interest. I hope you'll accept my desire not to say anything on that subject."

Please notice the "I" and "you." You get appreciation, I take responsibility for wanting to say nothing. If they ask again, you can reply again, maybe changing to, "I can see you're really interested, and I appreciate the interest, but I need to be okay with myself, so I'll still need to say nothing about it." If they persist (broken record technique), you can persist and use the same broken record.

You have a right to remain silent. Sure, there may be consequences and repercussions, but despite them, if you've decided you don't want to answer, then don't.

Be silent

That's right, be silent — say nothing.

This is different than "no comment" — you told them that you would not be answering. When being silent, you don't say that. In fact, you say nothing. You remain silent. It is possible that you are thinking about an answer. Ideally, the person who asks you the question will give you time to think about an answer.

But, if your questioner is like so many who ask questions but don't really want to know the answer, who just want to start a conversation, he or she will grab the ball and start talking, and guess what, you never will have had to answer the question. Silence works wonders with those people who ask questions and really don't want to know an answer. It works well with those people who ask questions as a method to tell you their story. It works well with impatient people. Their impatience will come to your rescue.

Remember of course what we stated earlier for the record: If you're comfortable answering the questions, there is no need to employ any option, just answer the question. You can paraphrase for understanding, if you want to, but, just answer the question. However, if you're just not feeling comfortable with the question, if you're wondering why the question is being asked of you or you feel the pressure and want time to think about an answer, you now have options.

Have you ever noticed that some people can get up in front of a group and seem to be able to field any and all questions, while other people virtually refuse such an assignment. Why?

Person number one knows his or her options. The person knows that no matter what the question, he or she can either answer or use any of the options available. That gives them the confidence to face the unknown because it's not an unknown when you're prepared. When you have options, they're prepared.

The three part question

We've learned to avoid asking a three part question but what if a three part is asked of you? Assuming you want to answer, how do you respond to avoid misunderstanding? Break it down. Just because they asked a single three part question doesn't mean you have to answer in kind. Unless your answer is yes to all three parts or no to all three parts. But if it isn't, and if you're asked, "Will you be able to check Mr. Jones' file before he comes in and if it isn't complete call him and reschedule his appointment with you for next Thursday?"

Break it down! "Yes, I will be able to check Mr. Jones' file before he comes in. Yes, I will be able to call him. But, no, I can't reschedule him for next Thursday. I'll be at an in-service that day. Is any other day acceptable?"

What three part questions are often asked of you? Be prepared. Note them now. Break them down now. Practice responding now so that when they're asked of you, you'll be ready.

The assumptive question

We've learned to avoid asking an assumptive question, but what if an assumptive question is asked of you? Assuming you want to answer, how do you respond to avoid being burdened by the assumption?

Suppose you were asked, "How could you close the lab without shutting down the incubator?"

You could try paraphrasing and say, "You mean you know for a fact that I closed the lab." This might help them recognize that they don't know that for a fact and they just assumed it, because you usually close down the lab.

You could try another version and say, "You mean you know for a fact that I didn't shut down the incubator?" This might help them recognize that maybe you did shut down the incubator and someone else came in after you and it was the other person who forgot to shut it down.

You could try "sounds like" and say, "Sounds like you know a lot more about what happened last night than I do. Why don't you fill me in on all the details."

You could treat the assumptive question like a multiple part question and break it down by saying, "I didn't shut down the incubator, because I wasn't the last person out. I didn't close the lab down. Have you checked with Robert?"

Notice when treating it as a multiple-part question, after you're done responding, ask a question yourself to get the questioner thinking about alternatives and remove the burden from you.

Another variation of the same type of response to this very same question might be, "When I left the lab, I closed it and shut down the incubator. If it was on, then someone must have come in after I left and done so. Any idea who that might have been?"

Again, notice when treating it as a multiple-part question, after you're done responding, ask a question yourself to get the questioner thinking about alternatives and remove the burden from you.

The negative question

We've learned to avoid negative questions. We're not grammarians, and we don't know if the other person is either. Negative questions are confusing. But, what if someone asks you a negative question. How do you respond? Remember "Robert, you're not in favor of the new vacation plan?"

Answer this in two parts:

1. Paraphrase it to the positive by saying, "You mean am I in favor?" They might respond "yes," or they might respond, "are you opposed?" But, whichever response, you've turned the question into a positive one.

2. Answer the question as your position dictates.
   You wouldn't ask a colleague this next question,
   because you know better, but suppose your colleague
   asks you, "Aren't you done with the chart?"

Answer it in two parts:

1. Paraphrase it to the positive by saying, "You mean, am
   I ready to relinquish the chart?" You've turned it into a
   positive-type question, with less room for misunderstanding.
2. Answer the question. Or if you choose, use an appropriate option skill like buying time.

Open or closed, yes or no, hidden motive or not, clear
question or confused, positive or negative, single or multiple,
they're all variables in the kinds of questions which others
can pose to you. Now you're prepared to deal with them all.

CHAPTER TWELVE

Silence

"Better to remain silent and be thought a fool than to speak out and remove all doubt."

Abraham Lincoln

Silence is golden. Everybody knows the maxim, but not everybody follows it. This is not to say there's no room for participation. We're coming to the end of a book which offers many techniques for saying what needs to be said in the best possible way, but no review of communication skills would be complete without the analysis of silence.

In essence there are three types of silence:

Active listening

The silence that is part of the skill of active listening. Please remember that "listen" and "silent" use the same six letters but they are not the same. Active listening does require silence to allow the other person to speak, but as they speak, as you silently listen, you are involved in their conversation.

Asking questions

The silence that is part of the skill of asking questions. Please remember that when you ask a question, since you really do want to know the answer you must remain silent until you get it. But here again, this silence does involve some action. In anticipation of their response you lean toward them, you show that you are interested and that you're waiting, but no sound fills the air; you are silent.

Think time

The silence that is part of "peace" and "think time." This silence is different than either of the other two because this silence is not part of a larger picture, not part of a skill. This silence is an entity unto itself. This silence allows you time to think, to gather your thoughts or to let your thoughts roam. It allows the other person time to think, to gather his or her own thoughts or to let those thoughts roam. Whenever people are discussing an issue, whether they are in agreement or disagreement, points are made that need reflection. There's no time to do this while you're speaking. There's no time to do this while the other person is speaking, so someone has to make the time for silence.

A technique which works well, utilizing the skills of "I" and "you," is the skill of buying time. Thus, when I realize that I just want "peace" time or "think" time, I'll say, "Robin, you've made some very interesting points, and I really need some time to reflect on them, so I'd like to ask for a 10 minute break, just to allow for think time. Okay?"

Now when I think, I don't have to look at anyone, or lean in any special way or make any verbal sounds of acknowledgment. I'm free to float in any direction I choose and be in whatever mode I need to allow myself to think. There are some people who need this time to think but they don't know how to ask for it. They haven't learned any of the skills you've learned so they struggle with it, trying to think while paying attention to what's going on. Or, worse yet, they go off into their own world of silence while the other person is talking and the other person doesn't get any active listening, the other person doesn't get any paraphrasing and the other person doesn't feel listened to and doesn't feel understood. No matter what kind of brilliant thoughts this "thinker" might eventually come up with, the speaker who felt neglected will not be a willing recipient of those ideas.

If you know such a person, help them, either by teaching them the skill or by buying silence for them. I have sometimes said, "Frank, I believe this is a complex issue that requires some considerable thought. May I suggest we give ourselves 10 minutes now to focus in on our own perspectives?"

The Franks of the world, who haven't learned the value of silence or how to buy time for it, will appreciate you all the more for what you've done.

Meetings

Silence represents a different situation at meetings. The larger the group, the easier it is to be silent, to get "lost," not say a word — not have to say a word. By itself this is fine. However, there are some people who like to "include" everyone and they'll not allow anyone to be silent. They say such things as, "We've not heard from you yet, Jacob. What do you think?"

Just because someone asks me to speak, just because someone asks me a question does not mean I need to answer, now or even later. Here's my chance to use any of the modules within the skill of responding to questions, especially the module on buying time.

I have often responded, "Harry, thank you for asking and seeking my input. You've helped me feel important. I appreciate it. By the same token, I'd rather not speak just to fill the air with sound. I need to know more, so I'll just sit back, listen and when I've got something to offer, I'll open up. Okay?" or,

"Harry, thank you for asking and seeking my input. You've helped me feel important. I appreciate it. But I'm in the middle of mulling over all that's been said so far, running it by some experiences of mine and I'm not done yet. I need some more time for thinking, so I hope I can just remain silent, do my thinking and when I'm ready to speak, I will. Okay?"

And then there are meetings when no one tries to include me and I just remain silent because I prefer it that way. Yet, I know that for some silence is interpreted as acquiescence or agreement. I've been at meetings when I've not said anything and two people who each saw an issue differently later told me individually that because I was silent they each thought I agreed with them. In other words, each person interpreted my silence to their own best interest. Since then I've learned that I cannot allow that misinterpretation so I take it upon myself somewhere during the meeting to say, "Lest my silence be interpreted for agreement or disagreement, let me say that my silence means neither. My silence means I'm thinking. I'm hearing everything you're saying, and I'm thinking."

At one time I thought that was enough. I was wrong. Now when I make that declaration, would you believe it, I ask for a reverse paraphrase, just so I can be sure one person in the room understood it and in their act of paraphrasing me, others hear it again?

"Silence is an act of peace, an act of calm, an act of reflection."

Silence is an act of peace, an act of calm, an act of reflection. It is a fitting conclusion to this book. It is also the hope of this author that you will now create a few minutes of silence to reflect on the skills you've learned, decide which skills you find most valuable and which skills still need your attention.

Epilogue

"Start talking — you've got
18 seconds until I interrupt."

"The only way you're going to solve problems is by communication."

Sir David Attenbourough

Some time ago I was asked by the editor of *Medicenter Management* magazine to write an article on "communications" with specific emphasis on front office personnel. The article entitled, "Front office personnel, first impressions count," appeared and created quite a stir.

In preparing and writing this article I interviewed many office managers and directors of medical centers. Virtually all agreed that front office personnel played a major role in the success of their organization. Most agreed that patients are affected as much, or more, by their treatment by the front office and paramedical personnel as by their physician. Most agreed that before the patient gets to see the doctor, the treatment that patient gets from personnel sets the stage for the mood they're in when they get to see their doctor. And finally, not only do first impressions count, but also last impressions count too, so it's the way the personnel say goodbye to this visit and set the stage for the next one, that helps determine whether this patient will be happy with their clinic and stay, or be unhappy and leave — even if the doctor's treatment has been satisfactory.

"Last impressions count too."

With such powerful consensus I expected that there would be strong action plans implemented to make sure that front office personnel and ancillary personnel received adequate training in an attempt to ensure that when they exerted their powerful role on the patient, it would be a positive exertion. How sad that only one of the many interviewed reported they had a plan for training their personnel on how to react and treat the patient. They all recognized that communication was essential, but nobody trained anybody. They all recognized that listening was important, but nobody trained anybody. They all recognized that the way a phone is answered is important but nobody trained anybody. They all recognized that the way someone's call is transferred, the way someone is put on hold, the way someone is told about anything are all important, but nobody trained anybody.

What did they do? They depended on the "common sense" of people. When they hired people they tried to hire people who liked other people. They tried to hire people with "outgoing personalities." They tried to hire people who could talk on the phone, who could smile, and then they admitted, they hoped and prayed that these people would adapt their normal nice personalities to the job.

If they determined the correct profile for success, and found people who met that profile, how sad that they provided no training to help them maximize their natural personality tendencies.

It almost appeared like the saying about the weather, "Everybody talks about the weather, but nobody does anything about it."

But that was not universal. One major medical institution challenged me to apply these skills in the hospital environment. We worked with the Respiratory Therapy Department. A study was formulated. Certain respiratory therapists (Group A) would receive basic communication training. Their training consisted of an overview of communication and its 13 skills, plus specific mastery training on active listening, buying time and paraphrasing.

In order to make this realistic, training was limited to two sessions, each two hours in duration with 10 days of practice between sessions. Other therapists (Group B) were selected, but not given the training.

After the training, a special team was assembled to follow up with the patients, from the therapists from Group A and Group B. The special team asked the patients about their reaction to their therapist:

"How well-understood did you feel when talking with your respiratory therapist?"

"How much do you think your respiratory therapist cares about you, personally?"

"How would you rate your treatment by your respiratory therapist?"

"Based on your treatment by your respiratory therapist, would you recommend this hospital to a friend if they needed treatment similar to yours?"

If by now you are a believer, you can predict the answers. After statistical analysis it was determined that:

- Patients of therapists in Group A felt better understood than patients of therapists in Group B;
- Patients of therapists in Group A felt better cared for than patients of therapists in Group B;
- Patients of therapists in Group A rated their treatment higher than patients of therapists in Group B; and

- Patients of therapists in Group A were far more likely to recommend the hospital to a friend than patients of therapists in Group B.

Is it any surprise that this department decided to train all members of their respiratory therapy staff?

Some directors of medical groups have attended Medical Group Management Association (MGMA) programs and heard one of my presentations and participated in certain exercises. They experienced this training themselves and invited me to work with their staff. Is it any surprise that they still extol the virtues of that training? Patients tell them they feel well treated when they come to their facility. Patients tell them they feel dignified, honored and respected when they come to their facility, and staff tells them, it's so easy. Now that they know what to do it's so easy, and the skill even carries over to their personal lives.

No, this is not a commercial, but I feel compelled to ask, "What kind of training do you provide for your staff to make sure that patients at your facility will feel good when they come in, feel good when they leave and be anxious to recommend your facility to others?"

There are changes in the wind. Not all patients are being treated like my wife's friend who complained bitterly to her, "My doctor never looks at me when I talk and then he's always rifling through papers which aggravates me. It's very frustrating!"

Not all patients are being treated like this one, as reported to me by an MGMA member. The patient was a woman doctor who was told by her doctor that she had breast cancer. And how did the treating physician notify his patient? He wrote her a note! He was afraid to face the patient and break the news.

On the other hand, medical publications are now publishing information such as:

"To most people, courtesy is best demonstrated by undivided attention, preferably that which is personalized as much as possible. Patients often complain that their physicians do not seek their input and too often do not listen to their descriptions."

"As the strongest indication that attention is being paid to the patient, the physician (and staff) should look and listen to the patient's description of his or her problem. Patients sense very quickly, though maybe incorrectly, that the physician who is writing in the chart and not looking at them is ignoring their problems."

It's wonderful that this information is being disseminated to the medical community. What is not being given equal space is what to do and how to do it.

However, even that issue is being addressed.

More than 30 years ago, Barbara M. Korsch, M.D., pioneered a method of teaching the then-unusual concept that a physician should treat the whole person, not just the problem. Until 1992, Dr. Korsch was head of General Pediatrics Division, Children's Hospital, Los Angeles, and Professor of Pediatrics at the University of Southern California Medical School.

She notes, "People think bedside manner is an inborn quality of nice, decent physicians. How can you teach compassion? Well, you can't teach compassion but you can teach techniques."

She teaches communication skills and then videotapes students while they examine patients and they watch the tapes to review their own performances.

An article about her concluded, "While Korsch says that virtually every medical school now has some version of a communication course, not all offer it as an integral part of the medical training. This she feels, misses the point: 'I believe that if residents are taught to communicate in a setting of care, it will be considered part of the care."

Another article in another publication goes on to list irritating listening habits. Some of them are:

"He never looks at me when I talk. I'm not sure he's listening."

"She continually toys with a pencil, paper or some other item when I'm talking. I wonder if she's listening."

"His poker face keeps me guessing whether he understands me or is even listening to me."

"When I am talking, she finishes sentences for me."

"He acts as if he is just waiting for me to finish so he can interject something of his own."

"He frequently looks at his watch or the clock while I am talking."

"She acts like she is doing me a favor in seeing me."

They are not describing behavior of health care professionals, but, does the shoe fit?

A consumer publication reports to its readers that they need to bridge the communication gap with their doctors. It reports that the average office visit lasts less than 15 minutes and that one study found that doctors interrupt patients' opening statement on average within 18 seconds of their arrival, often cutting patients off before they can communicate critical information.

The publication counsels its readers, "During the visit ask for time to talk. Mention at the outset that you have some questions. Then, politely insist on describing your main problems, fully, without interruption." It urges readers to become "assertive patients," to "take charge of your own health" and reports on at least five clinical trials, involving a total of more than 300 patients with a range of different ailments.

" ... over the next few months, the coached patients got much more information from their doctors than the uncoached patients and their health improved significantly. People with hypertension controlled their blood pressure more effectively, for example, and those with diabetes had lower blood-sugar levels."

The message seems clear — patients want to know. Patients want to have the right to ask and get answers. Patients want to be treated with dignity and respect. They'll read books, magazines and go to seminars to learn how to get it. That's wonderful, for the result will be a better informed patient with a better chance for better health. But, patients who do not get what they want from their existing medical facility, from their doctor and staff, will read and learn to go elsewhere.

As a final note, in a report from the *American Medical News*, the American Academy of Physician and Patient actually offers courses that teach the skills needed. The article refers to principles that underlie the academy's work today:

"There is more to meeting patients' needs than diagnosis and curing their diseases."

1. If you can't understand the patient's problem, you can't help the patient;
2. Good care is predicated on what patients, not physicians, need; and
3. There is more to meeting patients' needs than diagnosis and curing their diseases.

Remember back to the prologue and the needs of people? Fits perfectly, doesn't it?

The Academy reports it's not just the patient who benefits. Physicians who can't establish communication relationships with patients find themselves frustrated and dissatisfied with their patient encounters. But, one physician who learned the skills reported after returning to practice, "You begin to enjoy some parts of practicing medicine that many physicians find frustrating. You begin to take satisfaction in the routine, day-to-day work of a primary care physician."

So, it's truly win/win/win. The patient wins. The physician wins. And the practice wins. But it won't just happen. It won't even happen just because you've come to the end of this book. It will only happen if you will ask yourself, "Where do I fit in? What can I do today to practice one of the skills today? Who else can I work with? How can we implement this program within our entire organization?"

Then, with one person feeding on another, one person complimenting another when the skills are being observed in use, when reminding each other at missed opportunities, patients will notice the difference. They'll transmit their higher spirits to everyone and coming to work at a health care facility will be the full, rewarding kind of experience that only helping others with their health and well being can be.